Beginning Japanese workbook

Michael L. Kluemper • Lisa Berkson • Nathan Patton • Nobuko Patton

TUTTLE Publishing

Tokyo | Rutland, Vermont | Singapore

"Books to Span the East and West"

Tuttle Publishing was founded in 1832 in the small New England town of Rutland, Vermont [USA]. Our core values remain as strong today as they were then—to publish best-in-class books which bring people together one page at a time. In 1948, we established a publishing outpost in Japan—and Tuttle is now a leader in publishing English-language books about the arts, languages and cultures of Asia. The world has become a much smaller place today and Asia's economic and cultural influence has grown. Yet the need for meaningful dialogue and information about this diverse region has never been greater. Over the past seven decades, Tuttle has published thousands of books on subjects ranging from martial arts and paper crafts to language learning and literature—and our talented authors, illustrators, designers and photographers have won many prestigious awards. We welcome you to explore the wealth of information available on Asia at **www.tuttlepublishing.com**.

Published by Tuttle Publishing, an imprint of Periplus Editions (HK) Ltd.

www.tuttlepublishing.com

Illustrated by Keiko Murakami and Boya Sun

ISBN 978-0-8048-4558-8
Previously published under ISBN 978-0-8048-4057-6

Distributed by

North America, Latin America & Europe
Tuttle Publishing
364 Innovation Drive
North Clarendon,
VT 05759-9436 U.S.A.
Tel: 1 (802) 773-8930
Fax: 1 (802) 773-6993
info@tuttlepublishing.com
www.tuttlepublishing.com

Japan
Tuttle Publishing
Yaekari Building, 3rd Floor
5-4-12 Osaki
Shinagawa-ku
Tokyo 141 0032
Tel: (81) 3 5437-0171
Fax: (81) 3 5437-0755
sales@tuttle.co.jp
www.tuttle.co.jp

Asia Pacific
Berkeley Books Pte. Ltd.
3 Kallang Sector #04-01
Singapore 349278
Tel: (65) 6741-2178
Fax: (65) 6741-2179
inquiries@periplus.com.sg
www.tuttlepublishing.com

First edition
25 24 23 22   10 9 8 7 6 5 4   2212MP
Printed in Singapore

TUTTLE PUBLISHING® is a registered trademark of Tuttle Publishing, a division of Periplus Editions (HK) Ltd.

Contents

About *Beginning Japanese*

Welcome to the first level in a language learning series designed to give you a more natural experience in Japanese language acquisition.

The ***Beginning Japanese*** book, workbook, online audio recordings, and multimedia materials will help you to gain proficiency in the four aspects of language: speaking, listening, reading, and writing.

The Workbook is designed to help you check your understanding, and to allow you to practice and apply previously-learned and new material.

 Online audio recordings for the Listening Practice sections are available.

The web-based resource for this series, **TimeForJapanese.com**, contains additional learning content and practice tools. Visit it often!

To Download or Stream Audio Materials:

How to Download the Online Audio of this Book.
1. You must have an internet connection.
2. Type the URL below into to your web browser.

   https://www.tuttlepublishing.com/beginning-japanese-workbook

   For support, you can email us at info@tuttlepublishing.com.

名前：　　　　　　　　　　　　　　　　　日付：　　　月　　　日

❶ Practice the kanji below, tracing the first stroke in the first box, the first and second in the second box, etc. Fill in the other boxes with the complete *kanji*.

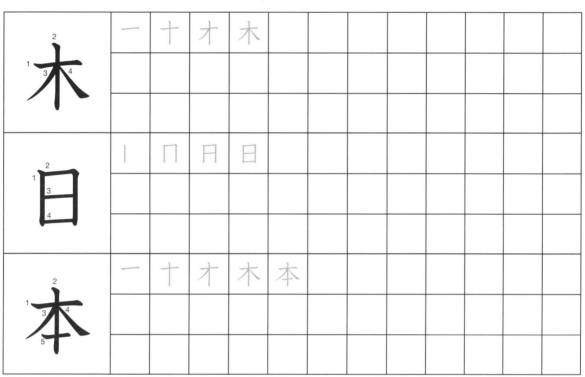

❷ Label each image, using Japanese (use *hiragana* where you've learned them).

1. _____   2. _____   3. _____

4. _____   5. _____   6. _____

Write the *kanji* stroke order below with the first stroke in the first box, the first and second stroke in the second box, etc. Fill in the remaining boxes in that row with the same *kanji*.

> For the *kanji* for "three" – 三, you would write the top (first) stroke in the first box, the first and second strokes in the second box, and the first through third strokes in the third box.
>
> | 三 | 一 | 二 | 三 | 三 | 三 | 三 | 三 | 三 | 三 | 三 | 三 | 三 | 三 |
> |---|---|---|---|---|---|---|---|---|---|---|---|---|---|

木													
本													
日													

名前：

日付：　　月　　日

➊ Practice the *kanji* below, tracing the first stroke in the first box, the first and second in the second box, etc. Fill in the other boxes with the complete *kanji*.

東	一	厂	冂	戸	申	車	東	東		
京	丶	亠	亠	古	古	京	京	京		
語	丶	二	三	言	言	言	訂	訐	語	語
	語	語								

➋ Label each image using Japanese.

1. _____ 2. _____ 3. _____

4. _____   5. _____   6. _____

 Write the correct Japanese classroom command under each drawing. Choose from among the expressions in the box.

7. _____   8. _____   9. _____

10. _____   11. _____   12. _____

(a) ひらいてください
(b) すわってください
(c) かいてください
(d) たってください
(e) よんでください
(f) とじてください
(g) きいてください
(h) だしてください
(i) みてください

13. _____   14. _____

四 Answer the questions below.

15. What part of speech usually comes at the end of basic sentences in Japanese?

   _____

16. What part of a Japanese sentence precedes the particle は?

   _____

17. How would you say this in Japanese: *Mr. Yamada is a teacher.*

   _____

五 Write the following in *kanji* or *hiragana* on the first blank. On the second blank, make them plural.

18. I, me   _____   _____

19. teacher   _____   _____

20. I (for males) _____   _____

六 List at least three occasions when Japanese people might bow.

21. _____

22. _____

23. _____

七 Write the *kanji* stroke order below with the first stroke in the first box, the first and second stroke in the second box, etc. Fill in the remaining boxes in that row with the same *kanji*. In the bottom row, practice writing whatever *kanji* you feel you need to practice the most.

東														
京														
語														

名前 ：

日付 ：   月   日

🔊 Listen to the prompts and circle the answers that best match the Japanese.

Choose the letter for the English that matches the spoken Japanese.

1. _____

2. _____

3. _____

4. _____

a. please write

b. please read

c. please listen

d. please stand up

e. please look

5. _____

6. _____

7. _____

8. _____

a. please stand up

b. please turn in/take out

c. please open

d. please sit down

e. please close

9. _____

10. _____

11. _____

12. _____

a. May I open?

b. May I sit down?

c. May I stand up?

d. May I look/see?

e. May I write?

名前：   日付：   月   日

 Practice the *kanji* below, tracing the first stroke in the first box, the first and second in the second box, etc. Fill in the other boxes with the complete *kanji*.

私	一	二	千	禾	禾	私	私					
父	ノ	ハ	父	父								
母	乚	口	口	母	母							

二 Fill in each blank with the correct Japanese word.

1. my mother _____

2. Tokyo _____

3. Japan _____

4. How do you do? _____

三 Fill in each blank with the correct Japanese word.

5. _____ 6. _____ 7. _____

8. _____   9. _____   10. _____

㊃ You will soon be introducing yourself and your family to your new Japanese friend. To help yourself remember what to say, write down each sentence here in Japanese.

11. How do you do?　　　　_____

12. This is my father.　　　_____

13. This is my mother.　　　_____

14. I am (*insert your own name*).　_____

15. Very pleased to meet you.　_____

㊄ Make the following statements into questions. Then answer each question using the negative, ではありません pattern. Remember to use a suffix indicating respect when talking about another person.

Statement	Question	Negative response
東京です。	16.	17.
やまもと先生です。	18.	19.
日本語です。	20.	21.
キアラさんです。	22.	23.

六 Jumble: The words in the sentences below are out of order. Re-order them to make grammatically-correct sentences in Japanese.

24. は　です　じゅん　私

_____

25. です　は　こちら　母

_____

七 Write the *kanji* stroke order below with the first stroke in the first box, the first and second stroke in the second box, etc. In the last row, write *kanji* that you feel you need to practice.

父												
母												
私												
東		ノ										
京												
語												

名前：　　　　　　　　　　　　　　　　　　　　日付：　　　　月　　　　日

➊ Practice the *kanji* below, tracing the first stroke in the first box, the first and second in the second box, etc. Fill in the other boxes with the complete *kanji*.

気　　ノ　ケ　气　気　気

元　　一　二　テ　元

人　　ノ　人

休　　ノ　イ　仁　什　仕　休

➋ Write the following words in Japanese using *hiragana* and *kanji* where you have been taught them.

1. I, me　　_____

2. my mother　　_____

3. meal　　_____

4. Good evening　　_____

⊜ Fill in each blank with the correct Japanese word.

5. good morning (polite)

    _____

6. good morning (casual)

    _____

7. I'm fine/energetic.

    _____

8. good night (polite)

    _____

9. good afternoon

    _____

10. How are you?

    _____

11. room

    _____

12. I'm home!

    _____

13. this

    _____

14. that

    _____

15. that over there

    _____

16. which

    _____

四 Respond with the appropriate Japanese word or expression to each situation below.

17. Greet your teacher before school.   _____

18. When someone returns home you say: _____

19. When you return home, you say: _____

20. You are eating a Japanese meal. You point to a small jar near you and ask if this is soy sauce.

    _____

21. Your friend is holding up a *hiragana* flash card. You ask if that is the *hiragana* "ka."

    _____

22. Someone away from you in the cafeteria has taken a suspicious white block-like piece of food and soy sauce out of her lunch bag. You ask your friend next to you if that over there is tofu.

    _____

23. It's three p.m. and you are shopping at the mall. You see a friend from your Japanese class. Greet your friend.

    _____

24. It is midnight and you have just finished working hard on your homework. You say good night to your parents.

_____

25. Your host father is offering you two food choices. You think they might be sushi, but you want to make certain. Ask him what they are, remembering to use the polite word for sushi.

_____

五 Write the *kanji* stroke order below with the first stroke in the first box, the first and second stroke in the second box, etc. In the last row, write *kanji* that you feel you need to practice.

元													
気													
人													
休													
父													
母													
私													

名前：   日付：   月   日

🔊 Listen to the prompts and circle the correct answers to the following questions.

1. What is the question being asked?
    a. Are you a student?   b. Are you Japanese?
    c. Are you American?   d. Are you a teacher?

2. What is the answer?
    a. Yes, that's right.   b. No, that's wrong.
    c. I do not know.   d. Please speak English.

3. What is the answer given to the question?
    a. Yes, that's right.   b. No, that's not right.
    c. I do not know.   d. Please speak English.

4. What is the question that is asked?
    a. Is this egg?   b. Is that near you an egg?
    c. Is this soy sauce?   d. Is that near you soy sauce?

5. What is the question that is asked?
    a. Is that near you an egg?   b. Is that over there an egg?
    c. Is this an egg?   d. Is that over there soy sauce?

6. What is the question that is being asked?
    a. Is this Japanese?   b. Is that Japanese?
    c. Is this Chinese?   d. Is that Chinese?

When do these conversations probably take place?

7. ____   a. morning
                                    b. afternoon
8. ____
                                    c. evening
9. ____   d. before sleeping.
                                    e. none of the above
10. ____

Where do these conversations probably take place?

11. ____   a. in a store
                                    b. in a house
12. ____
                                    c. in an airplane
                                    d. in a school

名前： | 日付： 月 日

➊ Translate the following words in Japanese.

1. How are you? _____

2. good night _____

3. chopsticks _____

4. east _____

➋ Fill in each blank with the correct Japanese word or phrase.

5. please stand up

   _____

6. well done, good job

   _____

7. I understand.

   _____

8. No, that's wrong.

   _____

9. please repeat

   _____

10. May I go to the bathroom?

    _____

11. please be quiet

    _____

12. May I get a drink?

    _____

13. Please listen

    _____

➌ You want to borrow several things from your Japanese friend. Ask each phrase in Japanese. Use *hiragana* and remember to use the honorific お prefix when appropriate.

例 FULLY EXAMPLE | Please loan me a book. 本を　かして下さい。

14. Please loan me the soy sauce.

    _____

15. Please loan me a pencil.

    _____

16. Please loan me some chopsticks.

    _____

17. Please loan me an egg.

    _____

18. Good job!

_____

④ Write the *kanji*, then the *hiragana* or *romaji* pronunciation for the word.

例 east _____東_____ ひがし HIGASHI
EXAMPLE

19. I/me   _____   _____

20. Japan   _____   _____

21. mother   _____   _____

22. father   _____   _____

23. healthy, energetic   _____   _____

24. Japanese person   _____   _____

25. (to) rest   _____   _____

⑤ Below is a short e-mail from a student, Satoshi. First, try to read the entire message. You may not understand every word, but do your best to comprehend the general idea. On the lines on the following page, write out as much of the message in *hiragana* as you can. For the underlined words, use *kanji*. Answer the questions at the end, in English.

KONNICHIwa。 OGENKI DESUka. WATASHIwa TAKEDA SATOSHI DESU。

CHICHIto HAHAto TOUKYOUni SUNDEIMASU。 WATASHIwa NIHONJIN

DESU。 WATASHIno EIGOno SENSEIno NAMAEwa SUZUKI SENSEI

DESU。 SUZUKI SENSEIwa TOTEMO II SENSEI DESU。 DEMO, SHUKUDAIo

TAKUSAN DASHIMASU。 IMAwa MOU GOZEN JUUNI JI DESU。 OSOI

DESU。 OYASUMINASAI。

_____

_____

_____

_____

_____

26. What is Satoshi about to do?

_____

27. What does Mrs. Suzuki teach?

_____

名前：　　　　　　　　　　　　　　日付：　　月　　日

🔊 Listen to the prompts and circle the correct answers to the following questions.

Choose the letter for the English that matches the spoken Japanese.

1. ___
2. ___
3. ___
4. ___

a. Please wait a moment.
b. Please say it one more time.
c. Please be quiet.
d. Please say it in English.
e. Slowly please.

5. ___
6. ___
7. ___
8. ___

a. May I drink water?
b. You did well.
c. How do you say it in Japanese?
d. May I go to the restroom?
e. May I go to my locker?

9. ___
10. ___
11. ___
12. ___

a. Please loan me a pen.
b. Yes, that's right.
c. No, that's not right.
d. Sit down.
e. Stand up.

名前： | 日付： 月 日

⚊ Practice the *kanji* below, tracing the first stroke in the first box, the first and second in the second box, etc. Fill in the other boxes with the complete *kanji*.

何	ノ	イ	亻	仁	伵	何	何			
家	﹅	宀	宀	宁	宁	字	字	家	家	
兄	﹅	冂	口	尸	兄					
姉	乀	女	女	女'	好	姉	姉	姉		
弟	丶	丷	凸	当	当	弟	弟			
妹	乀	女	女	女'	妒	妷	妹	妹		

二 Write the following in Japanese.

1. How do you do? _____   2. Japanese language _____

3. teacher _____   4. I, me _____

三 Assume that the family pictured here is your own family as you answer the questions below. Use as much *hiragana* and *kanji* as you can. Also try copying the names in *katakana*, noticing the differences in form and angularity as you do.

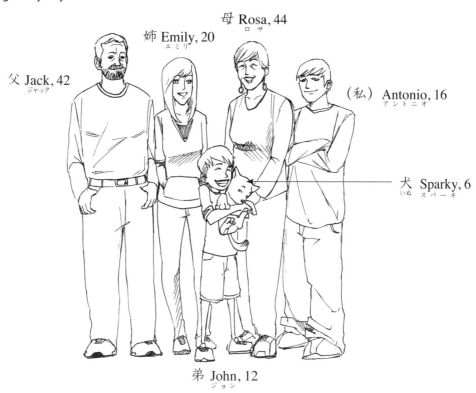

母 Rosa, 44
ロサ

姉 Emily, 20
エミリ

父 Jack, 42
ジャック

（私）Antonio, 16
アントニオ

犬 Sparky, 6
いぬ　スパーキ

弟 John, 12
ジョン

5. 家族は _____ です。 (#-人)
   ぞく

6-7. 私の_____は　42さいで、名前は_____です。
   なまえ

8-9. 私の_____は　20 (はたち)、名前は_____です。
   なまえ

10. 私の　名前は　_____ です。

11. _____は　いぬです。

12. 私の　母の　名前は　_____ です。

13–14. 私の　_____は　12さいで、名前は_____です。

Note: ～さい is the counter for age (____ years old).

四 Rewrite each phrase in Japanese. Be sure to use the particle の as shown in the example.

例 This is Mikiko's bag → <u>これは　みきこさんの　バッグです。</u>

15. This is my photograph.　　　　　　　　_____

16. That (near you) is my older sister's dog. _____

17. These are my father's chopsticks.　　　_____

18. That (over there) is my mother's book.　_____

19. That (near you) is my teacher's pen.　　_____

20. This is my little brother's cat.　　　　_____

五 You are showing your Japanese friend Satoshi a photograph of your family. USE YOUR OWN FAMILY TO ANSWER THE QUESTIONS. To say "I don't have one (or any)," use いません. Write each sentence in your best Japanese. On the second line, translate your answer into English.

21. さとし：ごかぞくは　何人ですか。

YOU　　：_____

(English)　_____

22. さとし：こちらは　だれですか。 (point at one family member)

YOU　　：_____

(English)　_____

23. さとし：お名前は？
　　　　　　　な まえ
YOU　　：_____

(English)　_____

24. さとし：ペットは　いますか。

YOU　　：_____

(English)　_____

六 Jumble: The words in the sentences below are out of order. Re-order them to make grammatically-correct sentences in Japanese.

25. それ　の　えんぴつ　か　は　先生　です

_____

26. さん人　は　です　家族
　　　　　　　　　　　　か　ぞく

_____

27. は　あれ　です　の　じゅんさん　いぬ

_____

28. 何　なまえ　は　か　です

_____

七 Write the *kanji* stroke order below with the first stroke in the first box, the first and second stroke in the second box, etc. In the last row, write another *kanji* from Chapter 1 that you feel you need to practice.

何														
兄														
姉														
妹														
家														
弟														
母														
父														
私														
東														

名前 : 　　　　　　　　　　　　　　　日付 :　　月　　日

● Practice the *kanji* below, tracing the first stroke in the first box, the first and second in the second box, etc. Fill in the other boxes with the complete *kanji*.

一	一										
二	一	二									
三	一	二	三								
四	丨	冂	冂	四	四						
五	一	丁	五	五							
六	亠	亠	六	六							

七	一	七										
八	ノ	八										
九	ノ	九										
十	一	十										
百	一	丆	丆	丆	百	百						

⊜ Write the following in Japanese, using *kanji* and *kana* (*hiragana* and/or *katakana*).

1. 10 people _____

2. Japanese person _____

3. I, me (male) _____

4. my younger brother_____

三 Write each number in both *kanji* and *kana* (*hiragana* and/or *katakana*).

5. 13 _____   6. 45 _____

7. 76 _____   8. 29 _____

9. 81 _____   10. 100 _____

四 Write the words for your own family members and then the words for someone else's family members. If you have finished learning *hiragana* (*hiragana* and/or *katakana*), write everything in *kanji* and *kana*. The first one is done for you.

English	My family	Someone else's family
father	父	お父さん
mother	11.	12.
older sister	13.	14.
older brother	15.	16.
younger sister	17.	18.
younger brother	19.	20.
grandfather	21.	22.
grandmother	23.	24.

五 Translate each sentence below into Japanese. When appropriate, be sure to use the family words for someone else's family. Plan ahead and think about which verb you have studied best fits each sentence (です, います, or あります).

> 例 EXAMPLE
> I have an older brother.　兄が　います。
> This is Jun's family.　こちらは　じゅんくんの　ごかぞく　です。

25. I have a mother and father. _____

26. There are two younger sisters (in someone else's family). _____

27. This is Ben's teacher. _____

28. Jun has 5 people in his family. _____

29. (I) have souvenirs (おみやげ). _____

六 Write the *kanji* stroke order below with the first stroke in the first box, the first and second stroke in the second box, etc. In the last rows, write *kanji* that you feel you need to practice.

十													
七													
九													
四													
何													
弟													
母													
父													
妹													
私													

名前 :

日付 :   月   日

● Practice the *kanji* below, tracing the first stroke in the first box, the first and second in the second box, etc. Fill in the other boxes with the complete *kanji*.

	一	ナ	大	犬							

● Write the following in Japanese, using *kanji* and *kana* (*hiragana* and/or *katakana*).

1. a friend's older brother _____

2. 45 people _____

3. my younger sister _____

4. my mother and father _____

● Translate each phrase into Japanese. Be sure to use the correct form of *this* ____ (この), *that* ____ (その), *that* ____ *over there* (あの), or *which* ____ (どの). Use *kanji* and *kana*.

5. this dog _____

6. that cat (near you) _____

7. this hat _____

8. this sushi _____

9. which sushi? _____

10. that teacher over there _____

11. those two people (near you) _____

12. that candy over there _____

④ Circle the expression that best fits each scenario below.

13. It's lunchtime and you are very hungry. Your classmate offers you one of her cookies. She says:
    a. クッキーを　どうぞ。
    b. クッキーを　ください。

14. You give your host mother the gift you brought her. You say:
    a. これを　どうぞ。
    b. これを　ください。

15. Your host brother offers you a rice ball. You accept and say:
    a. どうも　ありがとう。
    b. どういたしまして。

16. Your host mother has just returned home from work. You welcome her home by saying:
    a. ただいま。
    b. おかえりなさい。

17. You're going over to your friend's house. When you knock on the door, you say:
    a. しつれいします。
    b. おげんきですか。

18. You are introducing a family member to your new Japanese friend. You say:
    a. こちらは　父　です。
    b. これは　えんぴつ　です。

19. Your friend offers to share some candy with you. You thank her, and she then says:
    a. どうもありがとう。
    b. どういたしまして。

20. It's late and you are going to bed. You tell your host parents:
    a. おやすみなさい。
    b. おはようございます。

五 Jumble: The words in the sentences below are out of order. Re-order them to make grammatically-correct sentences in Japanese.

21. なまえ　の　は　妹さん　か　何　です

_____

_____

22. か　です　これ　何　は

_____

_____

23. を　おすし　ください

_____

_____

24. 何人　ごかぞく　か　は　です

_____

_____

名前：   日付：   月   日

🔊 Listen to the prompts and circle the correct answers to the following questions.

Natsumi, a Japanese high school student, is meeting Lisa, the New Zealand exchange student her family is hosting, for the first time in a car on the way from the airport to Natsumi's house.

1. How many people are in Lisa's family?
    a. 5   b. 6
    c. 7   d. 8

2. Who is Fluffy?
    a. Lisa's cat   b. Lisa's dog
    c. Natsumi's cat   d. Natsumi's dog

3. How many pets does Lisa introduce to Natsumi?
    a. zero   b. one
    c. two   d. nine

4. Why does Natsumi say that Lisa has nine members in her family?
    a. she counts pet(s)
    b. she includes herself in Lisa's family
    c. she includes both her own and Lisa's family
    d. her grandparents live with them

名前： | 日付： 月 日

⊖ Write the following expressions in Japanese, using *kanji* and *kana* (*hiragana* and/or *katakana*) where possible.

1. this candy _____

2. 124 _____

3. that teacher over there _____

4. friend's mother _____

⊜ Translate each sentence below into Japanese, using *kanji* and *kana* where possible.

> 例 Where is the pencil? えんぴつは　どこですか。

5. The pen is over there. _____

6. The chalk is over there, too. _____

7. Akira is there (near you). _____

8. Where is the teacher? _____

9. The teacher is here. _____

10. My friend is here too. _____

11. Please read the manga. _____

⊜ Use the expressions ～をどうぞ and ～をください to give away, or ask for, the following items, depending on whether you want the item for yourself or you want to give it to someone else. Then translate your sentences into English.

> 例 pencil えんぴつを　ください。
> Please give me a pencil.

12. chalk _____ _____

13. water _____ _____

14. eraser _____ _____

15. hat _____ _____

16. T-shirt _____ _____

17. dog _____ _____

18. notebook_____ _____

四 Fill in all the boxes by writing out the full *kanji* in each box until you get to the next *kanji*, then continue writing that *kanji*.

妹							兄							
姉							九							
私							人							
六							十							
休							百							
家							東							
京							語							
弟							犬							

名前：   日付：   月   日

● Write the following in Japanese, using *kanji* and *kana* (*hiragana* and/or *katakana*).

1. who _____ 2. where _____

3. 5 people _____ 4. a friend's grandfather _____

● Translate each Japanese sentence into English.

5. おなかが　ペコペコ　です。

_____

6. ばんごはんは　どこ　ですか。

_____

7. ばんごはんは　ここ　です。

_____

8. これは　たまご　ですか。

_____

9. はい、そう　です。

_____

10. それは　とうふ　ですか。

_____

11. いいえ、ちがいます。

_____

12. あれは　とうふ　です。　これは　ケーキ*　です。　どうぞ。
       け ー き

_____

* The long line in katakana doubles the preceding vowel sound. The ケ sound is doubled in this case.

三 Fill in all the boxes by writing out the full *kanji* in each box until you get to the next *kanji*, then continue writing that *kanji*.

語						母						
父						妹						
兄				五				七				

四 Draw a picture of a family with five or more members. Label each family member in Japanese and show each person holding at least one of the objects listed here. Use the list of Japanese names from the appendix.

> ねこ、犬、えんぴつ、ぼうし、あめ、たこ、まんが、たまご、お水（みず）、
> けしゴム（ごむ）、おすし、or おはし。

五 Write three sentences in Japanese about the drawing above.

13. _____

14. _____

15. _____

Write *kanji* above the **bold** words in the paragraph below. Then write as many *hiragana* as you can above all the other words.

HAJIMEMASHITE。 **WATASHI**no KAZOKUwa **YONIN** DESU。 **CHICHI**to **HAHA**to

OTOUTOto **WATASHI** DESU。 **HAHA**no NAMAEwa NANCY DESU。 **CHICHI**no

NAMAEwa CLARK DESU。 **OTOUTO**no NAMAEwa JORDAN DESU。 **WATASHI**wa

CLARA DESU。 INUmo IMASU。 INUno NAMAEwa SPOT DESU。 DOUZO

YOROSHIKU ONEGAISHIMASU。

名前：

日付： 月 日

🔊 Listen to the prompts and circle the correct answers to the following questions.

A teacher asks Jordan some questions in class.

1. What is the first question the teacher asks?
   a. Who is in the classroom?   b. What is here?
   c. What is your name?   d. Where are you from?

2. What object does Jordan NOT mention having?
   a. a blackboard   b. pencils
   c. pens   d. erasers

3. Who/what is in the picture?
   a. Mr. Yoshida and his older brother   b. Jordan's older brother and the dog
   c. Mr. Yoshida and his older sister   d. Jordan's older sister and the dog

4. What is way over there?
   a. a hat   b. a picture of a dog
   c. a picture of a cat   d. a bag

5. How does Jordan feel at the end?
   a. tired   b. nervous
   c. hungry   d. full

名前：　　　　　　　　　　　　　　　　　　　　　　日付：　　　月　　　日

① Practice the *kanji* below, tracing the first stroke in the first box, the first and second in the second box, etc. Fill in the other boxes with the complete *kanji*.

高	丶	二	广	亠	亠	咅	高	高	高	高	
小	亅	小	小								
中	丶	冂	口	中							
大	一	𠂇	大								
学	丶	丷	丷	丷	学	学	学				
校	一	十	才	木	杉	朾	栌	栌	杉	校	

年	ノ	⺧	⺡	午	乍	年							
先	ノ	⺅	⺧	生	牛	先							
生	ノ	⺅	⺧	牛	生								
山	丨	山	山										

⊜ Write the following words using *kanji* and *hiragana*.

1. my mother _____

2. that pencil over there _____

3. dinner _____

4. an empty stomach says _____

⊜ Place an ✕ (ばつ) on the line if the statement is false and ◯ (まる) if the statement is true, based upon your current situation.

5. ____ きょうかしょが あります。

6. ____ けしゴムが あります。
ごむ

7. ____ いい本が あります。

8. ____ あめが あります。

9. ____ ねこが います。

10. ____ おじいさんが います。

11. ____ 日本語の 先生が います。

12. ____ 弟さんが います。

名前：   日付：   月   日

➖ Rewrite the following in Japanese. Use as many *kanji* as you can, including the *hiragana* (*furigana*) pronunciation above each *kanji*.

1. Akiko is a 6th grader.   _____

2. Jack is an 11th grader.   _____

3. Ken is a college freshman.   _____

4. Ben is a 9th grader.   _____

5. Emi is a 5th grader.   _____

6. I am a/an ___ grader.   _____

7. Miyazaki is a math teacher.   _____

8. My mother is a teacher.   _____

⚌ Fill in the blanks in each sentence below, using the cues in parentheses and the correct verb forms for: います／あります・いません／ありません. Use *hiragana* or 漢字.

> **例** いぬが ＿います。(dog, exists)

9. 妹さんは_____か。(exists, is there)

10. _____は _____。(teacher, is not there)

11. ベン君の _____は どこですか。(mother)

12. _____は _____に _____。(my father, at home, is not there)

13. _____が _____。(eraser, there is)

三 Unscramble the words below, writing each sentence correctly in 日本語. Then translate each into 英語.

> 例 私　これ　です　は　の　ぼうし
>
> 日本語：これは　私の　ぼうしです。
>
> 英語　：This is my hat.

14. 中学　妹　です　年生　一　は

　　日本語：_____

　　英語　：_____

15. Kiara（キアラ）　はじめまして　どうぞ　です　よろしく　(3 sentences)

　　日本語：_____

　　英語　：_____

16. います　お母さん　は　か　どこ　に

　　日本語：_____

　　英語　：_____

四 Fill in the blanks with the correct Japanese word.

17. しゅんいちさんの　ぼうしは　(very)_____　(big)_____ です。

18. 先生の　かばんは　(a bit)_____ (large)_____です。

19. あの　いぬの　みみ (ears) は　(very)_____ (small)_____です。

20. ももこさんの　ふでばこ (pencil case) は　(little)_____です。

五 Tomoko, a student in Japan, has many questions about you and your life. Use full sentences to reply to her letter to you in Japanese. Include a greeting (for example, こんにちは or はじめまして). Be sure to answer all of Tomoko's questions. Use います/いません and あります/ありません.

こんにちは、友子です。

しつもんが あります。あなたに お兄さんは いますか。妹さんは いますか。あと、弟さんは いますか。それと、おばあさんは いますか。それに、犬は いますか。
　漫画は ありますか。下敷は ありますか。えんぴつと けしゴムは ありますか。日本語の 辞書は ありますか。それと、家族の 写真は ありますか。

では。

_____

_____

_____

_____

_____

_____

_____

_____

六 Write the *kanji* stroke order below with the first stroke in the first box, the first and second stroke in the second box, etc. Fill in the remaining boxes in that row with the same *kanji*.

高														
小														
中														
大														
学														
校														
年														
生														
山														
先														

名前：   日付：   月   日

⊖ Practice the *kanji* below tracing the first stroke in the first box, the first and second in the second box, etc. Fill in the other boxes with the complete *kanji*.

英	一	十	艹	艹	芢	苙	英	英			
国	丨	冂	冂	冂	囝	国	国	国			
音	丶	亠	立	产	立	产	音	音	音		
楽	丶	亻	白	白	白	泊	泊	泊	渔	楽	楽
	楽										
今	ノ	人	今	今							
分	ノ	八	分	分							

● Write the following words using *kanji* and *hiragana*.

1. high school _____   2. 4th grader_____

3. blackboard _____   4. (friend's) little brother _____

● For each of the following *kanji*, write in the *hiragana* on the top line and the English below it. Refer to the textbook's New Words list in section 3.2.

5. 科学   6. 数学   7. 体育

(H) _____   _____   _____

(E) _____   _____   _____

8. 英語   9. 国語   10. 美術

(H) _____   _____   _____

(E) _____   _____   _____

● Translate the following into Japanese. Refer to the classroom commands and classroom objects pages in your textbook if necessary. Use the particle を.

11. Please open (your) textbooks. _____

    _____

12. Please write (it).   _____

    _____

13. Please listen.   _____

    _____

14. Please get out paper.   _____

    _____

15. Please close your books.   _____

    _____

16. Please read the kanji.   _____

    _____

名前： 日付： 月 日

⚫ Fill in the chart below with your weekly class schedule, in 日本語. Place an ✕ through the boxes you don't need. If your class schedule is the same each day, start with Monday and fill in each box; by the time you get to Thursday, try to write all your classes from memory. For Friday, write in an ideal schedule.

	月 (Mon)	火 (Tue)	水 (Wed)	木 (Thu)	金 (Fri)
1					
2					
3					
4					
5					
6					
7					

⚫ Write the following times using *kanji* and *kana* (*hiragana* and/or *katakana*).

1. 1:40 _____

2. 2:39 _____

3. 3:00 _____

4. 4:07 _____

5. 5:30 _____

6. 6:00 _____

7. 7:00 _____

8. 8:47 _____

9. 9:00 _____

10. 10:00 _____

11. 11:51 _____

12. 12:01 _____

⚫ Translate each of the following sentences into Japanese. Be careful to first determine if the time expression is specific (needing the particle に) or general.

例 At 6:30, please open the door. 六時半に　ドアを　あけてください。

13. Tomorrow please watch television. _____

14. Every day I have English class. _____

15. At 11:30, please shut the door. _____

四 Jumble: The characters for the sentences below are out of order. Place them in the correct order.

16. は　小学生　の　妹　ありません　私　では
(My younger sister is not an elementary student.)

_____

17. 時　います　分　二　校　七　に　学　十　に　は　私　(I am in school at 7:20.)

_____

18. は　学　です　年　中　生　私　三　(I am a ninth grader.)

_____

19. と　と　と　が　あります　日本語　音楽　びじゅつ　きょう　しゃかい
(Today I have music and art and Japanese and social studies.)

_____

五 Write the *kanji* stroke order below with the first stroke in the first box, the first and second stroke in the second box, etc. In the final row, write a *kanji* which you have already learned, but need to practice. Fill in all of the boxes in each row with completed *kanji*.

英													
国													
音													
楽													
今													
分													

名前：　　　　　　　　　　　　　　　　日付：　　　月　　　日

➖ Practice the *kanji* below, tracing the first stroke in the first box, the first and second in the second box, etc. Fill in the other boxes with the complete *kanji*.

書	フ	ヲ	ョ	ヨ	彐	聿	書	書	書	書		
寺	一	十	土	土	寺	寺						
時	l	�𠆢	日	日	日一	日十	旷	昨	時	時		
門	l	冂	冂	尸	尸	門	門	門				
間	l	冂	冂	尸	尸	門	門	門	門	間	間	間
下	一	丁	下									

⊜ Write the following using *kanji* and *hiragana*.

1. Tokyo University   _____

2. English   _____

3. There are 4 people in my family. _____

4. There is no dog.   _____

5. Please write kanji every day. _____

⊜ Use the schedule below to answer the following questions.

～時	時間目	授業 じゅぎょう
8:00～8:55	一時間目	国語
9:00～9:20	休み	
9:20～10:15	二時間目	体育 たいいく
10:20～11:15	三時間目	英語
11:20～12:15	四時間目	音楽
12:15～1:05	ひる休み	
1:05～2:00	五時間目	科学 かがく
2:05～3:00	六時間目	美術 びじゅつ
3:00～	放課後 ほうかご	部活動 ぶかつどう

6. 一時間目は　何　ですか。

   _____

7. 五時間目は　何　ですか。

   _____

8. 六時間目は　何　ですか。

   _____

9. 体育は　何時間目　ですか。
    たいいく

   _____

10. 音楽は　何時間目　ですか。

   _____

11. 英語は　何時間目　ですか。

_____

12. 部活動は　何時から　ですか。
　　ぶかつどう

_____

㊃ Write the *kanji* stroke order below with the first stroke in the first box, the first and second stroke in the second box, etc.

書												
寺												
時												
門												
間												
下												

㊄ Answer the following in Japanese using complete sentences.

┌───┐
| 例 　What time does your Japanese class start? |
| れい |
| EXAMPLE 　日本語　は　八時三十五分　から　です。 |
└───┘

13. What time does school start?

_____

14. What time does your English class start?

_____

15. Write what time you will start to eat dinner this evening.

_____

16. What time is third period?

_____

名前：   日付：   月   日

🔊 Listen to the prompts and choose the correct answers to the following questions.

Terry, an exchange student in Japan who has recently arrived from Ireland, and Naoko, a Japanese high school student, discuss their school schedules and school clubs.

Based on Terry's schedule, match the letter with the correct period.

1. _____ 1st period   a. Physical Education (P.E.)

2. _____ 2nd period   b. art

3. _____ 3rd period   c. Japanese

4. _____ 4th period   d. math

5. _____ 5th period   e. history

6. What is Terry's club?
   a. karate
   b. kendo
   c. baseball
   d. tea ceremony

7. The gym is:
   a. hot
   b. cold
   c. old
   d. new

8. Terry thinks his club is:
   a. easy but kind of boring.
   b. hard but fun.
   c. hard and boring.
   d. hot but fun.

名前：　　　　　　　　　　　　　　　　日付：　　　月　　　日

● Practice the *kanji* below, tracing the first stroke in the first box, the first and second in the second box, etc. Fill in the other boxes with the complete *kanji*.

		丶	冂	冂	曰	旦	早	昇	暑	暑	暑	暑
暑												
		丶	ﾉ丶	宀	宀	宁	守	宭	宭	宭	寒	寒	寒
寒												
		丶	㇈	㇈	ネ	ネ	初	初	初	神			
神												
		丶	㇈	㇈	ネ	ネ	社	社					
社												

● Write the following words using *kanji* and *hiragana*.

1. one o'clock _____

2. middle school _____

3. every day _____

4. please write _____

● Translate each statement into Japanese. Use でも at the beginning of the second sentence.

5. There are 3rd year high school students. But there are no first year high school students.

_____

_____

6. There is a basketball club. But there is no chorus club.

_____

_____

7. There is a sixth period. But there is no seventh period.

_____

_____

8. The gymnasium is hot. However, the library is cool.

_____

_____

9. The classrooms are muggy. However, the computer lab is cold.

_____

_____

四 Restate the following in Japanese. Refer to your classroom commands if you need help.

10. Please write with pencil. _____

11. Please say it in English. _____

五 Write the *kanji* stroke order below with the first stroke in the first box, the first and second stroke in the second box, etc.

暑														
寒														
神														
社														

名前：   日付：   月   日

● Practice the *kanji* below tracing the first stroke in the first box, the first and second in the second box, etc. Fill in the other boxes with the complete *kanji*.

風	ノ	几	凡	凡	凨	凬	風	風	風			
友	一	ナ	方	友								

● Write the following in Japanese using *hiragana* and *kanji* where you have learned them.

1. math _____

3. temple _____

2. It's hot, isn't it? _____

4. 3rd period _____

● Translate each sentence into Japanese using ね at the end.

5. This is a junior high school, right?

   _____

6. You are in your second year of high school, aren't you?

   _____

7. There are no teachers, are there?

   _____

8. It's muggy, isn't it?

   _____

9. My high school is hot. But my younger sister's elementary school is cool, isn't it?

_____

四 Translate each sentence into Japanese using よ at the end.

10. (I am telling you), there is no brass band club.

_____

11. (Hey, listen up), it's cold.

_____

12. My math class is fun!

_____

13. (Listen up), 5th period is art class.

_____

14. (Let me inform you), this is the baseball club.

_____

五 Write the *kanji* stroke order below with the first stroke in the first box, the first and second stroke in the second box, etc.

風														
寒														
妹														
弟														
書														
国														
友														

名前 :   日付 :   月   日

🔊 Listen to the prompts and mark each statement with ◯（まる）if it is true, or ✕（ばつ）if it is false.

Melissa, a studious high school exchange student from Australia, and Hiroshi, a Japanese high school student, discuss plans for the rest of the day.

1. _____ Hiroshi has history and math homework.

2. _____ Melissa has Japanese homework.

3. _____ Hiroshi has club activities today.

4. _____ Hiroshi wants to study after school at home.

5. _____ Melissa likes the place because it has air conditioning.

6. _____ Hiroshi can go to the shrine.

名前：	日付： 月 日

Write the *kanji* above the **bold** words. Then write the *romaji* above all the other letters. Rewrite this paragraph in English.

けんじくんと　さおりさんは　**こうこうせい**です。けんじくんも

さおりさんも　**にねんせい**です。**いちじかんめ**の　じゅぎょうは

えいごです。びじゅつは**ろくじかんめ**です。それから、すうがくと

しゃかいと　かがくと　こくごも　あります。でも、**おんがく**の

じゅぎょうは　ありません。さおりさんのクラブは　バスケ　です。
　　　　　　　　　　　　　　　く ら ぶ　　　　　　　　　ば す け

けんじくんの　クラブは　やきゅうぶです。バスケも　やきゅうも
　　　　　　　　く ら ぶ

たのしいです。

_____

_____

_____

_____

_____

_____

_____

_____

名前：   日付：   月   日

● Practice the *kanji* below tracing the first stroke in the first box, the first and second in the second box, etc. Fill in the other boxes with the complete *kanji*.

言

外

● Write the Japanese words for the clues in *hiragana* in the puzzle.

Down
1. a Chinese person
2. an English person
3. a German person
4. the United States of America
5. a Dutch person
9. to say

Across
2. Indonesia
6. France
7. South Korea
8. a foreign person
10. Spain

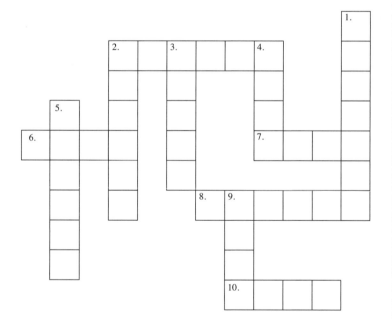

Write the following words using *kanji* and *kana* (*hiragana* and/or *katakana*).

11. to say _____

12. China and Korea _____

13. foreign country _____

14. foreign person _____

15. high school _____

16. middle school _____

17. mother _____

18. father _____

四 Match the maps with the names of the countries.

19.

20.

21.

22.

A. アメリカ
　あ　め　り　か

B. メキシコ
　め　き　し　こ

C. 中国
　ちゅうごく

D. 韓国
　かんこく

E. ロシア
　ろ　し　ぁ

F. ドイツ
　ど　い　つ

G. 台湾
　たい　わん

H. インドネシア
　い　ん　ど　ね　し　ぁ

23.

24.

25.

26.

五 Write the following in English.

27. _____ 私は　日本から　です。

28. _____ 父は　中国人　です。

29. _____ 先生は、「こんにちは。」と　言いました。

30. _____ 山本さんは、「私は　韓国人　ではありま
　　　　　　　　　　　　　　やまもと　　　　　　　　かん
　　　　せん。」と言いました。

31. _____ お父さんは　インドネシア人　ですか。
　　　　　　　　　　　　　　　　　　　　い　ん　ど　ね　し　ぁ

名前：	日付：	月	日

➊ Use complete sentences to write an appropriate question or answer in Japanese based upon fact.

1. お母さんは　何人 (なにじん) 　ですか。 _____

2. 日本語の先生は　何人　いますか。 _____

3. _____アメリカ人 (あめりか) 　です。

4. _____父は　日系人 (にっけい) 　です。

5. _____母は　中国系 (けい) と　韓国系 (かんこくけい) 　です。

➋ Use complete sentences in Japanese to tell what nationality at least three people you know are. Try to write their names in *katakana* if they do not have a Japanese name or use their title/relationship to you such as 先生、母、兄、etc.

6. _____

7. _____

8. _____

➌ Where you have learned the *kanji*, cross out the *hiragana* and write the *kanji* above.

9. そのひとは　外こくじん　です。 　　That person is from a foreign country.

10. おとうさんは　にほんじん　です。 　　His/her father is Japanese.

11. わたしは、「こんにちは。」と　いいました。 　I said "hello."

12. わたしは　こうこういちねんせい　です。 　I am a tenth grader.

13. いもうとは　ちゅうがくさんねんせい　です。 　My younger sister is a ninth grader.

14. ははは、せんせい　ではありません。 　　My mother is not a teacher.

15. ともだちは、ちゅうごくじん　です。 　　My friend is Chinese.

16. えみこさんは、だいがくにねんせい　です。 　Emiko is a second year college student.

④ Natalia needs some help. Write a self introduction for her in Japanese as if you were her, including as many vocabulary words and *kanji* as you can. Also, be sure to include introductory and closing remarks. Begin with "はじめまして。"

Natalia (ナタリア) is an American. She has five people in her family. Natalia's mother is Russian. However, Natalia's father is French. She has a younger brother and an older sister. Natalia is in her first year of high school.

_____

_____

_____

_____

_____

_____

_____

⑤ Write the *kanji* stroke order below with the first stroke in the first box, the first and second stroke in the second box, etc. (You might have leftover boxes after you've completely written the *kanji*.) In the last row, write another *kanji* from a previous chapter that you feel you need to practice.

言													
外													

名前：	日付：	月	日

➊ Write the following words using *kanji* and *kana* (*hiragana* and/or *katakana*).

1   to speak/talk _____

2.   foreign person _____

3.   foreign country _____

4.   my older sister _____

➋ Practice the *kanji* below tracing the first stroke in the first box, the first and second strokes in the second box, etc. Fill in the other boxes with the complete *kanji*.

話	、	ニ	二	三	三	言	言	言	言	訂	訂	話
話												

➌ For each nationality below, write what language people from that country commonly speak. Answer in full sentences like the one in the example.

> **例** フランス: <u>フランス人　は　フランス語　を　話します。</u>
> ふらんす

5. 中国人   : _____
    ちゅうごくじん

6. スペイン人   : _____
    すぺいんじん

7. ロシア人   : _____
    ろしあじん

8. 日本人   : _____
    にほんじん

9. オランダ人   : _____
    おらんだじん

10. ポルトガル人 : _____
    ぽるとがるじん

11. 韓国人   : _____
    かんこくじん

12. イタリア人   : _____
    いたりあじん

13. ドイツ人   : _____
    どいつじん

14. アメリカ人   : _____
    あめりかじん

四 Write the main language spoken in each of the countries below on the corresponding lines.

15. _____   16. _____   17. _____

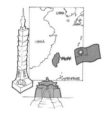

18. _____   19. _____   20. _____

五 Write the *kanji* stroke order below with the first stroke in the first box, the first and second stroke in the second box, etc. Write the full *kanji* in the remaining boxes for that row. In the last row, write another *kanji* from a previous chapter that you feel you need to practice.

話														

名前：   日付：   月   日

① Practice the *kanji* below tracing the first stroke in the first box, the first and second in the second box, etc. Fill in the other boxes with the complete *kanji*.

食	ノ	八	𠆢	今	今	今	食	食	食			
飲	ノ	𠆢	𠆢	今	今	含	食	食	食	飲	飲	飲
物	ノ	┗	牛	牛	牛	物	物	物				
車	一	厂	冂	百	百	亘	車					

② Following the example sentences, write about a language you speak and three sentences about languages you and others do not speak.

例
EXAMPLE
私　は　ドイツ語　を　話します。イタリア語　は　話しません。

1. _____

2. _____

3. _____

4. _____

三 Assuming you can only order one item from those below, for number 8 write a sentence about one thing you will drink and for numbers 9 through 11 write sentences about three things you will not drink.

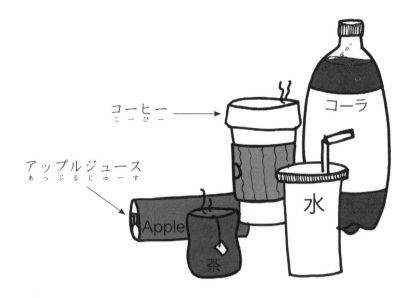

コーヒー
こ ー ひ ー

コーラ

アップルジュース
あ っ ぷ る じ ゅ ー す

Apple

水

茶

例 私は　おちゃを　飲みます。お水は　飲みません。
れい
EXAMPLE　　　　　　　　　　　　　　　　　みず

5. _____

6. _____

7. _____

8. _____

四 Fill in the correct particles.

9. キアラ _____ 学校 _____ 食べます。
Kiara eats at school.

10. じゅん _____ 家 _____ 手伝います。
てつだ
Jun helps out at home.

11. 明子さん_____ 図書館_____ お水_____ 飲みます。
あきこ　　　　　　　　としょかん　　　　　　みず
Aiko drinks water in the library.

12. ベン君_____ 大学_____ 日本語_____ 勉強します。
べんきょう
Ben will study Japanese in college.

五 Jumble: The words in the sentences below are out of order. Re-order them to make grammatically-correct sentences in Japanese.

13. 話します　は　を　英語　弟
    (My little brother speaks English.)

    _____

14. 何語　お母さん　話します　を　は　か
    (What language does your mother speak?)

    _____

15. 何人　は　けんさん　か　です
    (What nationality is Ken?)

    _____

16. と　を　話します　か　お母さん　お父さん　は　何語
    (What languages do your father and mother speak?)

    _____

17. です　えみさん　外国人　は
    (Emi is a foreign citizen.)

    _____

六 Write the *kanji* stroke order below with the first stroke in the first box, the first and second stroke in the second box, etc. Write out the full *kanji* in the remaining boxes in each row. In the last row, write another *kanji* from a previous chapter that you feel you need to practice.

食											
飲											
物											
車											

名前：   日付：   月   日

➊ Practice the *kanji* below tracing the first stroke in the first box, the first and second in the second box, etc. Fill in the other boxes with the complete *kanji*.

行	ノ	ク	彳	行	行	行					
来	一	一	口	立	平	来	来				
帰	）	）	）	）	）	）	）	）	）		

➋ Write the following words using *kanji* and then *hiragana*.

1. to go _____   2. to come _____   3. to return (home) _____

_____   _____   _____

➌ Translate the following.

4. I go to the bakery.   _____

5. Dad returns home at 5:00.   _____

6. Jun will come to Tokyo.   _____

7. I will go to Japan with my teacher. _____

四 Write the *kanji* stroke order below with the first stroke in the first box, the first and second stroke in the second box, etc. Write the full *kanji* in the remaining boxes in each row. In the last row, write another *kanji* from a previous chapter that you feel you need to practice.

行											
来											
帰											

五 Write the *kanji* that you can above the *hiragana*. Cross out only the *hiragana* that you are replacing. Then translate each sentence into English.

8. じゅん君は　こうこういちねんせい　です。でも　ベン君は　ちゅうがくさんねん
せい　です。

_____

9. れいこさんは　ちゅうごくごを　はなします。

_____

10. 友さんは、「ほんやさんは　あそこに　あります。」と　いいました。

_____

六 Jumble: The words in the sentences below are out of order. Re-order them to make grammatically-correct sentences in Japanese.

11. 学校　明日　来ます　に　は　母　(My mother will come to school tomorrow.)
あした

_____

12. へ　日本　帰ります　は　友さん　(Tomo will return to Japan.)

_____

13. じゅん君　私　と　は　へ　行きます　中国　(Jun and I will go to China.)
くん

_____

14. は　東京　へ　行きます　私　(I will go to Tokyo.)

_____

名前：　　　　　　　　　　　　　日付：　　月　　日

➊ Practice the *kanji* below tracing the first stroke in the first box, the first and second in the second box, etc. Fill in the other boxes with the complete *kanji*.

見	丨	冂	冂	月	目	貝	見				
聞	丨	冂	冂	尸	尸	門	門	門	門	門	門
聞	聞										

➋ Fill in the blanks in the verb chart below, using *kanji* and *kana* as needed.

non-past (~ます)	non-past negative (~ません)	英語	verb type (Type 1 or う) (Type 2 or る) (irregular)
あります			Type 1 or う
		to exist, animate	
	食べません		
	話しません		Type 1 or う
言います			
		to help out	
分かります			
来ます(きます)			

☰ Complete each sentence using both affirmative and negative verb endings for each of the following. Write your own sentences for the last two.

> 例
> EXAMPLE
>
> スペインへ　　行きます。
> すぺいん
> スペインへ　　行きません。
> すぺいん

1.　朝ご飯を _____。
　　あさ　はん

　　朝ご飯を _____。
　　あさ　はん

2.　家へ _____。

　　家へ _____。

3.　本屋へ _____。
　　　や

　　本屋へ _____。
　　　や

4.　お水を _____。
　　　みず

　　お水を _____。

5.　宿題を _____。
　　しゅくだい

　　宿題を _____。
　　しゅくだい

6.　本を _____。

　　本を _____。

7.　学校へ _____。

　　学校へ _____。

8.　友達と _____。
　　ともだち

　　友達と _____。

9.　_____。

　　_____。

10.　_____。

　　_____。

㉔ Write the correct *kanji* and *kana* for each word or phrase.

11. please listen _____ 12. foreign person _____

13. please say _____ 14. to speak _____

15. drinks _____ 16. to go _____

17. to return (home) _____ 18. foods _____

㊄ Write the *kanji* stroke order below with the first stroke in the first box, the first and second stroke in the second box, etc. Write the full *kanji* in the remaining boxes in each row. In the last row, write another *kanji* from a previous chapter that you feel you need to practice.

見											
聞											

㊅ Write *kanji* above the underlined *hiragana*.

キアラさんは　じゅん君と　<u>こうこう</u>へ　<u>い</u>きます。教室に

<u>せんせい</u>が　います。キアラさんの　<u>がっこう</u>は　<u>たの</u>しい　です。

放課後、キアラさんと　じゅん君と　ベン君は、　<u>じんじゃ</u>へ　いきます。その

じんじゃの　鳥居は　<u>とき</u>の　<u>もん</u>　です。そこに　<u>おおかぜ</u>が　きます。

名前：   日付：   月   日

🔊 Listen as one person tells the other what she will do tomorrow. Place the items in the correct order.

Choose the letter to match the correct order in which the person will do things in the morning.

1. _____   a. go to a friend's house

2. _____   b. read a book

3. _____   c. eat breakfast

4. _____   d. listen to the radio

5. _____   e. write an essay for homework

Choose the letter to match the correct order in which the person will do things in the afternoon.

6. _____   a. return home in the evening

7. _____   b. eat dinner

8. _____   c. drink green tea

9. _____   d. eat lunch with his friend

10. _____   e. help mother

名前：	日付：　　月　　日

一 Write the following times in *kanji* and *kana*.

1. 1:40 ____________________ 2. 2:39 ____________________

3. 3:00 ____________________ 4. 4:07 ____________________

5. 5:15 ____________________ 6. 6:07 ____________________

7. 7:00 ____________________ 8. 8:30 ____________________

9. 9:20 ____________________ 10. 10:00 ____________________

11. 11:00 ____________________ 12. 12:00 ____________________

二 Practice the *kanji* below tracing the first stroke in the first box, the first and second in the second box, etc. Fill in the other boxes with the complete *kanji*.

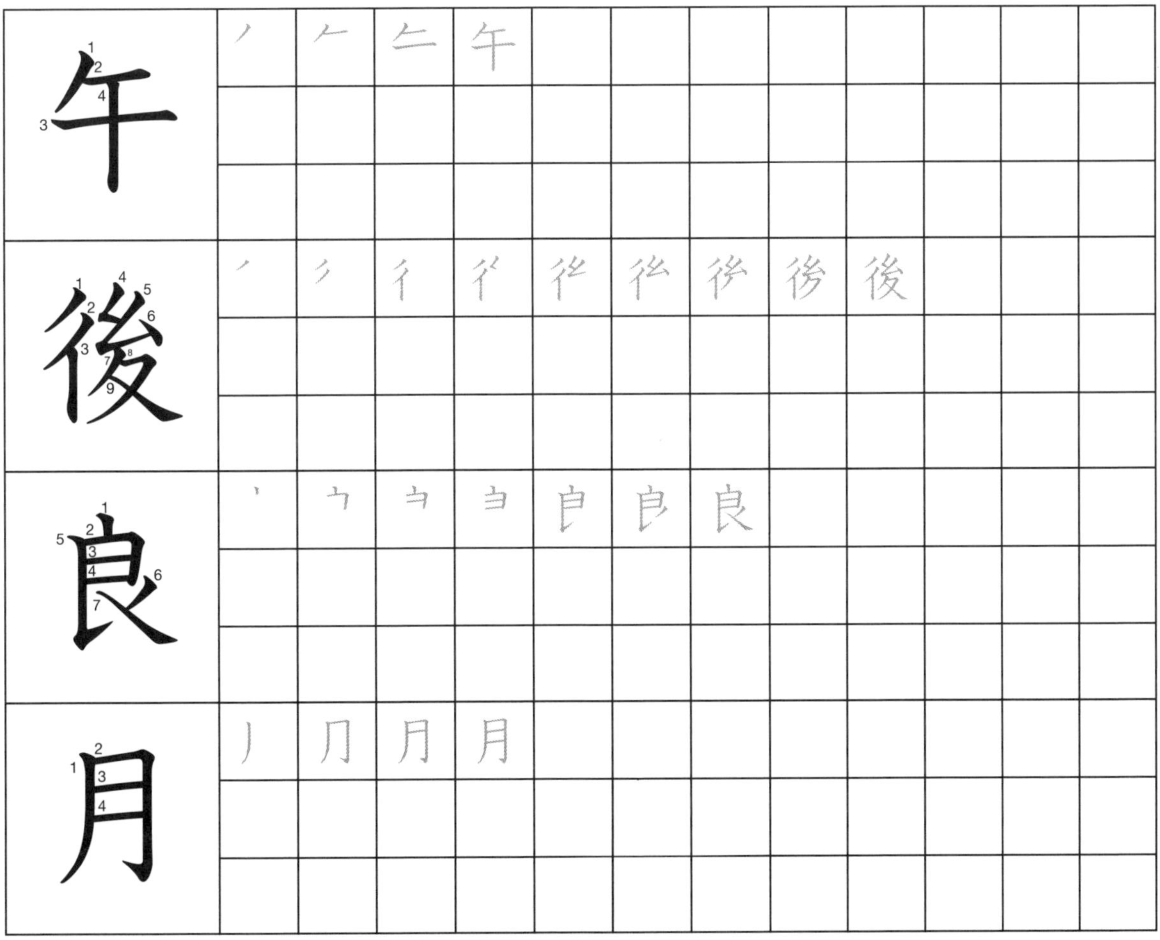

火	、	゛	少	火								
水	ﾉ	기	水	水								
金	ノ	八	스	合	仐	釒	金	金				
土	一	十	土									
曜	l	冂	日	日	旷	旷	旷	町	明	曜	曜	曜
	曜	曜	曜	曜	曜	曜						

Write the following days of the week using *kanji* and *kana*.

13. Sunday _____   14. Monday _____

15. Tuesday _____   16. Thursday _____

17. Friday _____   18. Saturday _____

四 Translate the following dialogue into English.

19. みわ　　: 土曜日に　パーティーが　あります。来て下さい。

_____

20. さとし: 何時　ですか。

_____

21. みわ　　: 一時です。ぎょうざを　*作ります。
　　　　　　　　　　　　　　　　つく

_____

22. さとし: そう　ですか。僕は　ぎょうざは　ちょっと・・・・
　　　　　　　　　　　　　ぼく

_____

23. みわ　　: 二時に　ケーキを　食べます。ドイツの　ケーキ　です。
　　　　　　　　　　け ー き　　　　　　　ど いっ　　　け ー き

_____

24. さとし: ケーキ　ですか。いい　ですね。じゃあ、　僕も　パーティーへ
　　　　　　　け ー き　　　　　　　　　　　　　　　　　　ぼく
　　　　　　行きます！

_____

* 作ります – to make
　つく

五 Write the *kanji* stroke order below with the first stroke in the first box, the first and second in the second box, etc. Write the full *kanji* in the remaining boxes in each row.

月													
火													
水													
金													
分													
年													
後													

名前：　　　　　　　　　　　　　　　　　　　　日付：　　　　月　　　　日

● Practice the *kanji* below tracing the first stroke in the first box, the first and second in the second box, etc. Fill in the other boxes with the complete *kanji*.

千	ノ 二 千						
末	一 二 キ オ 末						
毎	ノ ト 仁 勺 匈 毎						
週	ノ 几 月 円 用 周 周 周 调 调 週						

● Write the following verbs in the affirmative past tense.

1. 行きます _____
2. 帰ります _____
3. 言います _____
4. 始めます _____
   　はじ
5. 来ます _____
6. 終わります _____
   　お

▤ Write the following verbs in the negative past tense.

7. 起きます _____
   お

8. います _____

9. 寝ます _____
   ね

10. 話します _____

11. あります _____

12. 手伝います _____
   てつだ

▥ Write the following in *kanji* and then again in *hiragana*.

13. May _____

14. October _____

15. Sunday _____

16. Wednesday _____

▦ Write the following sentences in Japanese.

17. Kiara came to Japan on Tuesday.

_____

18. I returned to the U.S.A. on Thursday.

_____

19. Ben did not sleep on Saturday.

_____

20. I did not go to Tokyo.

_____

▧ Answer the following questions in Japanese.

21. お母さんは　何月生まれ　ですか。

_____

22. あなたは　何月生まれ　ですか。

_____

23. 先生は　何月生まれ　ですか。

_____

24. 友達は　何月生まれ　ですか。

_____

七 Jumble: The words in the sentences below are out of order. Re-order them to make grammatically-correct sentences in Japanese.

25. テレビ　七時　に　見ます　を　(I will watch television at 7:00.)

_____

26. 三時半　帰ります　に　午後　へ　家　毎日　(I go home at 3:30 p.m. every day.)

_____

27. 行きます　大阪　友弘さん　八月　へ　に　は　(Tomohiro will go to Osaka in August.)
　　　　　　　　ともひろ

_____

28. は　を　飲みました　くみ子さん　コーラ　(Kumiko drank a cola.)

_____

八 Write the *kanji* stroke order below with the first stroke in the first box, the first and second stroke in the second box, etc. Write the full *kanji* in the remaining boxes in each row.

末														
毎														
千														
金														
分														
年														
後														

名前：　　　　　　　　　　　　　　　　日付：　　月　　日

一 Write the following dates in *kanji* and *kana*.

1. May 23　_____

2. June 2　_____

3. October 31　_____

4. July 4　_____

二 Write the following in Japanese.

5. from 1:00 until 3:00　_____

6. from Monday until Friday　_____

7. from June until August　_____

8. from Wednesday until Saturday _____

三 Write the following in Japanese.

9. I did not eat anything from 8:00 until 5:00.

_____

_____

10. Aiko did not drink anything from Friday until Sunday.

_____

_____

名前：　　　　　　　　　　　　　　　　　日付：　　　月　　　日

🔊 Listen to the prompts and choose the best responses to the following questions.

1. What time is it now?
   a. 10:00 a.m.   b. 11:00 a.m.
   c. 10:00 p.m.   d. 11:00 p.m.

2. What time will the second speaker go to sleep?
   a. 10:00 a.m.   b. 10:30 p.m.
   c. 11:00 p.m.   d. 11:30 p.m.

3. What time will the second speaker wake up?
   a. 5:00 a.m.   b. 5:30 a.m.
   c. 6:00 a.m.   d. 6:30 a.m.

4. What are the starting and ending times of the school?
   a. 8:00-3:00   b. 8:15-3:50
   c. 8:15-3:15   d. 7:45-2:45

5. What is the birth date of the second speaker?
   a. November 25, 1994   b. October 25, 1995
   c. September 15, 1994   d. August 15, 1995

名前：　　　　　　　　　　　　　　　　　　　　　　日付：　　　　月　　　　日

➊ Practice the *kanji* below, tracing the first stroke in the first box, the first and second in the second box, etc. Fill in the other boxes with the complete *kanji*.

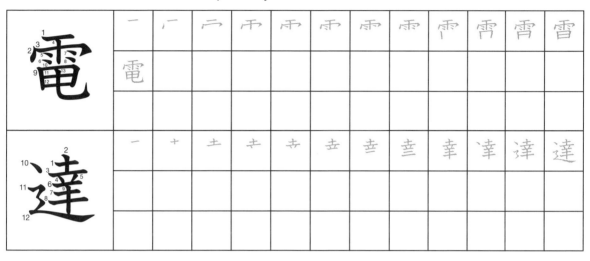

➋ Write the following in Japanese using *kanji* and *hiragana*.

1. next month _____

2. last Thursday _____

3. every year _____

4. September 2, 1945 _____

➌ Write the following in Japanese using *kanji* and *hiragana*.

5. I was at my grandmother's house from last Tuesday until this Thursday.

_____

6. I go to school from Monday until Friday.

_____

7. I will study from tomorrow until Sunday.

_____

8. My mother studied in Japan from 2002 until 2008.

_____

9. Every week, I study Japanese.

_____

10. Next year I will go from Tokyo to New York (ニューヨーク).

_____

11. Yesterday, I walked from 8 a.m. until 9 a.m.

_____

12. Last Saturday, my mother and I played Ping-Pong from 2:30 p.m. until 3:45 p.m.

_____

四 Write the *kanji* stroke order below with the first stroke in the first box, the first and second stroke in the second box, etc. Write the full *kanji* in the remaining boxes in each row.

週													
末													
電													
気													
達													
金													
曜													

BEGINNING JAPANESE WORKBOOK

5-5 Activities

名前：　　　　　　　　　　　　　　　　　日付：　　月　　日

⊖ Use Japanese to answer these questions about yourself and your schedule. Answer in complete sentences and use as many 漢字 as you can.

1. 何年　生まれですか。　＿＿＿＿＿＿＿＿＿＿＿＿＿＿＿

2. 何月　生まれですか。　＿＿＿＿＿＿＿＿＿＿＿＿＿＿＿

3. 誕生日は　いつですか。　＿＿＿＿＿＿＿＿＿＿＿＿＿

4. 毎日　何時に　起きますか。＿＿＿＿＿＿＿＿＿＿＿＿

5. 昨日　晩ご飯に　何を　食べましたか。

　　＿＿＿＿＿＿＿＿＿＿＿＿＿＿＿＿＿＿＿＿＿＿＿＿＿

6. 今日　の　朝　何を　飲みましたか。

　　＿＿＿＿＿＿＿＿＿＿＿＿＿＿＿＿＿＿＿＿＿＿＿＿＿

7. 英語の　授業は　何時から　何時まで　ですか。

　　＿＿＿＿＿＿＿＿＿＿＿＿＿＿＿＿＿＿＿＿＿＿＿＿＿

8. 冬休み(winter break)は　何月何日から　何月何日までですか。

　　＿＿＿＿＿＿＿＿＿＿＿＿＿＿＿＿＿＿＿＿＿＿＿＿＿

⊜ Fill in the blanks below with time words so that the statements are true according to Kiara's journal entries for Chapter 5.

9. キアラさんは　先週の　＿＿＿＿＿＿＿　に　学校に　行きました。(5-1)

10. ＿＿＿＿＿＿＿の　金曜日に　大風が　ありました。(5-1)

11. 先週の　土曜日に　＿＿＿＿＿＿＿＿＿へ　行きました。(5-1)

12. 長崎から　奈良の　東大寺まで　＿＿＿＿＿＿時間　かかりました (took)。(5-1)

13. ＿＿＿＿＿＿＿＿年に　奈良に　着きました。(5-2)

14. 一月二十日の　午後＿＿＿＿＿時二十分に　＿＿＿＿＿を　見ました。(5-2)

15. 友さんは　＿＿＿＿＿＿＿＿＿　たくさんの　食べ物を　食べました。(5-3)

BEGINNING JAPANESE WORKBOOK 85

☰ Translate the following sentences.

16. 来週の　水曜日は　私の　誕生日です。_____
   たんじょうび

17. 十一月十日生まれです。_____

18. 私は　千九百九十一年　生まれです。_____

19. 午前六時から　午後十二時まで　忙しいです。_____
   いそが

20. 毎日　朝ご飯に　卵を　食べます。_____
   あさ　はん　たまご

21. 来週土曜日の　誕生日パーティーで　チョコレートケーキを　食べます。
   たんじょうび　ぱ ー てぃ ー　ちょこれ ー とけ ー き

   _____

22. 友達は　午前十一時に　来ます。そして、ダンスを　します。カラオケも　しま
   だ ん す　　か ら お け
   す。

   _____

23. 私の　誕生日　パーティーへ　どうぞ！
   たんじょうび

   _____

四 Jumble: The words in the sentences below are out of order. Re-order them to make grammatically-correct sentences in Japanese.

24. から　です　学校　まで　は　三月　四月　(School is from April until March.)

   _____

25. 来ました　から　長崎　本　この　は　(This book came from Nagasaki.)
   ながさき

   _____

26. だれ　でした　バスケ　しません　昨日　も　を
   ば す け　　　きのう
   (Yesterday, no one played basketball.)

   _____

27. 横浜　先月　行きました　へ　(Last month I went to Yokohama.)
   よこはま

   _____

名前：　　　　　　　　　　　　　　　　日付：　　月　　日

🔊 Listen to the prompts and choose the best responses for the following questions.

1. What is the first speaker's question?
   a. What did you do last Sunday?
   b. What will you do next Sunday?
   c. What did you do last Saturday?
   d. What will you do next Saturday?

2. What does the second speaker say about the festival?
   a. He has gone every year for the last 10 years.
   b. He went last year but will not go this year.
   c. He did not go last year but will go this year.
   d. He will never go to the festival.

3. What time is the festival open?
   a. 6:00-8:00 a.m.
   b. 6:00-9:00 a.m.
   c. 6:00-8:00 p.m.
   d. 6:00-9:00 p.m.

4. What will be the meeting point for the two speakers?
   a. 5:30 a.m. at the shrine
   b. 6:30 a.m. at the school
   c. 5:30 p.m. at the shrine
   d. 6:30 p.m. as the school

名前：   日付：   月   日

⊖ Practice the *kanji* below, tracing the first stroke in the first box, the first and second in the second box, etc. Fill in the other boxes with the complete *kanji*.

体	ノ	イ	仁	什	休	休	体					
目	l	冂	冄	月	目							
口	l	冂	口									
耳	一	T	F	F	王	耳						
手	ノ	二	三	手								
足	丶	冂	口	甲	早	昆	足					

心	ヽ	心	心	心							
持	一	十	扌	扩	扩	抹	拝	持	持		
待	ノ	ク	彳	彳	彳	彳	往	待	待		
強	⁊	⁊	弓	弘	弘	弘	弘	弘	強	強	強

Write the following using *kanji* and *kana*.

1. legs are long _____

2. hands are small _____

3. to write _____

4. ten o'clock _____

Jumble: the sounds for several body parts are jumbled below. Write the correct word, and the *kanji*, if you know it, in the blanks.

例 EXAMPLE　おか　<u>かお</u>　顔

5. たまあ _____ _____

6. おかな _____ _____

7. しあ _____ _____

8. ちく _____ _____

9. せい _____ _____

10. ころこ _____ _____

11. なは _____ _____

12. たか _____ _____

名前：   日付：   月   日

⊖ Draw a picture of a person and label as many body parts as you can, using both *hiragana* and *kanji*.

⊜ Translate each sentence into Japanese using as many *kanji* as possible.

1.   My mother's eyes are big.

_____

2.   My younger sister's ears are small. But (she) has good hearing (ears).

_____

3.   My little brother's feet are big. But (his) eyes are small.

_____

4.   My judo teacher is strong.

_____

5.   Today is Monday. I will go to judo class.

_____

≡ Use Kiara's journal in Chapter 6.1 to answer these questions, in English.

6. Who did Kiara, Ben, and Jun meet?

_____

7. Why is the person Kiara, Ben, and Jun met famous?

_____

8. Why was the city of Hiraizumi famous in the 12th century?

_____

9. What sort of invitation did Kiara, Ben, Jun, and Tomo receive? From whom? What was the special occasion?

_____

_____

10. Briefly describe some general details of a legend or folktale you know, trying to include as much Japanese as you can. You may then write more in English.

_____

_____

_____

_____

_____

_____

_____

_____

_____

名前：　　　　　　　　　　　　　　　　　　　　　　日付：　　　月　　　日

🔊 *Two high school students discuss their family members.*

1. How many family members are there?

   _____

2. Write a sentence describing at least one physical characteristic of the mother.

   _____

3. Write a sentence describing at least one physical characteristic of the father.

   _____

4. Write a sentence including at least two characteristics of the older brother.

   _____

5. Write a sentence including at least two characteristics of the younger sister.

   _____

6. What is said about the grandmother?

   _____

7. What is a characteristic of the grandfather?

   _____

名前：　　　　　　　　　　　　　　　日付：　　　月　　　日

● Practice the *kanji* below, tracing the first stroke in the first box, the first and second in the second box, etc. Fill in the other boxes with the complete *kanji*.

医	一	丆	丆	医	医	医	医				
者	一	十	土	耂	耂	者	者	者			
薬	一	十	艹	艹	艹	苎	苩	苩	苩	蓮	蓮	蓮
	蓮	蓮	薬	薬							

● Write the following in Japanese.

1.　My friend is sick.　_____

2.　My mother had a fever.　_____

3.　I have a cold.　_____

4.　My friend is in the hospital. _____

● Write the following sentences in Japanese using the ～ても　いい　です(か) pattern.

5.　May I eat?　_____

6.　May I go to Japan?　_____

7.　You may open your books.　_____

8.　You may drink water.　_____

四 Write the following in Japanese using the ～ては　いけません pattern.

9.　You may NOT stand up. _____

10.　You may NOT sleep at 9:00 p.m. _____

11.　You may NOT drink sake. _____

12.　You may NOT go to the bathroom. _____

五 Write the following in Japanese. Be sure to include the particle で (*by means of*).

13.　You may speak in Japanese. _____

14.　You may come to school by bicycle (じてんしゃ). _____

15.　You may write in English. _____

六 Pretend that an exchange student from Japan who speaks absolutely no English is arriving to your school. To help her, in the space below write four sentences about things you can do in your school and four sentences about things you may not do. Use verbs from the charts in textbook Chapter 6.2.

_____

_____

_____

_____

_____

_____

_____

_____

名前：   日付：   月   日

● Practice the *kanji* below, tracing the first stroke in the first box, the first and second in the second box, etc. Fill in the other boxes with the complete *kanji*.

着	、	｀	丷	丷	丷	羊	羊	羊	着	着	着	着

● Write the following in Japanese.

1. Western style clothes _____

2. to wear on the head _____

3. to wear above the waist _____

4. to wear below the waist _____

● Draw a picture of a man and woman based on the descriptions here. Include all the details given.

Woman: 背が 高い です。足が 長いです。やせて います。かみが 長い です。目が 大きい です。ぼうしを かぶって います。シャツを 着ています。スカートを はいて います。靴を はいて います。靴下を はいて います。

Man: 背が低い です。足が 短いです。太って います。かみは ありません。耳が 小さい です。ジャケットを 着て います。パンツを はいて います。靴下を はいて います。でも、靴は はいていません。

四 Write the following in Japanese using the ～て　います pattern.

5. My friend is wearing a kimono. _____

6. Kiara is sleeping. _____

7. Tomo is eating sushi. _____

8. Yuki is wearing glasses. _____

9. Naomi is wearing a necklace. _____

10. Ken is wearing a hat. _____

五 Write the following in Japanese using the ～て　いません pattern.

11. Akio is not wearing a shirt. _____

12. I am not studying. _____

13. Kumi is not wearing a ring. (ゆびわ) _____

六 Some of your friends and family are very predictable. In the space below, write five sentences about what you are sure they are doing right now. Use the ～て　います and ～て　いません patterns.

_____

_____

_____

_____

_____

名前 :　　　　　　　　　　　　　　　　　　　　　日付 :　　　　月　　　　日

🔊 Listen to the prompts and choose the best responses for the following questions.

A mother and her teenage daughter discuss what the daughter can and cannot wear to a party.

1. Does the mom give her daughter permission to wear the first shirt that her daughter asks about?

   _____ Yes   _____ No

2. Does the mom give her daughter permission to wear the second shirt that her daughter asks about?

   _____ Yes   _____ No

3. Whose shoes does the daughter want to wear?
   a. her sister's shoes   b. her brother's shoes
   c. her mother's shoes   d. her friend's shoes

4. Does the mom give permission to wear those shoes?

   _____ Yes   _____ No

5. Does the mom give permission to wear her diamond necklace?

   _____ Yes   _____ No

6. Does the mom give permission to wear her gold necklace?

   _____ Yes   _____ No

7. By what means of transportation does the daughter want to go to the party?
   a. her friend's car   b. taxi
   c. limousine   d. her own car

8. By what means of transportation does the mother plan to take her daughter to the party?
   a. her friend's car   b. taxi
   c. limousine   d. her own car

名前 :　　　　　　　　　　　　　　　　　　日付 :　　　月　　　日

➖ Write the following using *kanji*, *kana*, and particles if necessary.

1.　is studying　　　　　_____

2.　is wearing pants　　　_____

3.　Tuesday at 4:25 p.m.　_____

4.　please read　　　　　 _____

➖ Translate each sentence into Japanese using *kanji* where appropriate.

5.　Ken'ichi wakes up and eats breakfast.

　　_____

6.　Ken'ichi is extremely tall. But his ears are a little small.

　　_____

7.　Hiroshi goes to school by bus, goes to class, and talks to friends.

　　_____

8.　At 12:20, Ken'ichi eats lunch at the cafeteria.

　　_____

9.　After school, Ken'ichi goes to the library, reads a magazine, and uses (つかいます) the computer.

　　_____

10.　At 8 p.m., Ken'ichi and Sara went to Kazuhiro's house.

　　_____

11.　Kazue's mother will make (つくります) a cake and write a card (カード). Tomorrow is Kazue's birthday!

　　_____

三 Write five sentences in Japanese describing what the people below are wearing. Then label as many body parts as you can.

_____

_____

_____

_____

_____

四 Read the clues and solve these two riddles about well-known personalities. Write your answers in English.

12. 僕は　とても　ふとっています。ひげが　あります。髪の毛が　長いです。
いつも　スーツを　きています。１２月２５日に　たくさんの　子供に　プレゼ
ントを　持って行きます。僕は　だれですか。

_____

13. 私は　動物です。耳が　長くて、二つ　あります。しっぽ(tail)も　あります。毎
日　外に　います。レタスと　人参(carrots)を　よく食べて、お水を　飲みます。
子供の　家に　たまごと　チョコレートを　持って行きます。四月うまれです。
私は　だれですか。

_____

名前 :   日付 :   月   日

🔊 Listen to the prompts and choose the best responses for the following questions.

Two teenage girls (one is Sayaka, the daughter from the previous listening practice) talk at a party.

1. What does Sayaka use to write her name on the name tag?
    a. pencil   b. pen
    c. marker   d. crayon

2. What two things does Sayaka's friend say are over there (あちら)?
    a. presents and toys   b. balloons and games
    c. food and drink   d. swimming and dancing

3. What does Sayaka's friend say is delicious?
    a. sushi   b. ice cream
    c. tenpura   d. sweets

4. What are the four things that Sayaka's friend wants to do with everyone?
    a. eat, drink, chat, and play games
    b. eat, drink, watch videos, and sing karaoke
    c. eat, drink, swim, and open presents
    d. eat, drink, play games, and watch movies

5. What time will the party end?
    a. 6 p.m.   b. 8 p.m.
    c. 9 p.m.   d. 10 p.m.

6. According to Sayaka's friend, what is everyone NOT allowed to do until the party ends?
    a. leave   b. open presents
    c. eat cake   d. sing songs

名前：　　　　　　　　　　　　　　　　　　日付：　　　月　　　日

一 Practice the *kanji* below, tracing the first stroke in the first box, the first and second in the second box, etc. Fill in the other boxes with the complete *kanji*.

花	一	十	艹	艹	花	花	花				
池	丶	氵	氵	汋	汕	池					
趣	一	十	土	キ	キ	走	走	走	赺	赺	赺
	趣	趣	趣								
味	丨	口	口	叮	叮	吽	味				
事	一	一	一	彐	写	写	写	事			

㊁ Translate the following using *kanji* and *kana*.

1. Ken has short hair. _____

2. Reiko is tall. (height) _____

3. Every day, I listen to music. _____

4. Tomoko's mother sometimes drinks tea. _____

㊂ Change each ～ます verb into the dictionary form + 事こと. Then write the English definition.

～ます **form**	dictionary (infinitive) form + 事こと	英語
食べます	食べる 事こと	eating
寝ね ます		
踊おど ります (to dance)		
書きます		
読よ みます		
飲みます		
歌うた います		
勉強べんきょう します		
練習れんしゅう します		

㊃ Make sentences about hobbies using the cues. Use as many 漢字 as possible. Refer to the example below when making your sentences.

例れいEXAMPLE	Hanako	singing	花子さんの 趣味は 歌を 歌う事 です。うた

5. Emi   sleeping   _____

6. Taro   reading books   _____

7. Kousuke   dancing   _____

8. Kazumi   video games   _____

9. Hiro   not piano   _____

10. Keisuke   not football   _____

11. Chizuko   studying English. _____

五 Write a short (5-6 sentence) paragraph about your family or close friends and their hobbies. Remember to use the words for your own family members (父, 母, etc.). Use as many 漢字 as possible.

_____

_____

_____

_____

_____

_____

_____

_____

_____

_____

六 Write the *kanji* stroke order below with the first stroke in the first box, the first and second stroke in the second box, etc. In the last rows, write other *kanji* from a previous chapter that you feel you need to practice.

花											
趣											
味											
池											
事											

名前：	日付：	月	日

● Practice the *kanji* below, tracing the first stroke in the first box, the first and second in the second box, etc. Fill in the other boxes with the complete *kanji*. Use the last rows to practice other *kanji* you have learned.

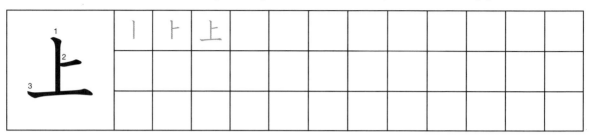

● Write the following sentences in 日本語. Use as many 漢字 as you can.

1. My big brother likes milk (ミルク).

_____

2. My mother is a little good at baseball.

_____

3. My friend is very good at karate.

_____

4. Dad is not good at kendo.

_____

5. Mrs. Yamada is a little bad at judo.

_____

6. My mother is good at singing, but my father is not.

_____

三 Refer to the textbook's New Words list in section 7.1. Categorize at least twelve of these hobbies in the circles below based on whether you like, dislike, or feel neutral about them. Then, write two sentences about hobbies that you like, and two sentences about hobbies you dislike.

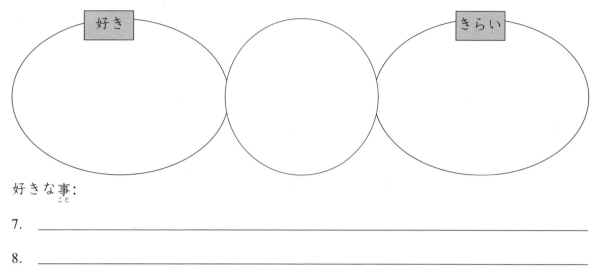

好きな事:
<small>こと</small>

7. _____

8. _____

きらいな事:
<small>こと</small>

9. _____

10. _____

四 Read the sentences below and use が to combine each pair into one sentence in 日本語. Model your sentences on the example here. Use each at least once: とくい, にがて, じょうず, and へた.

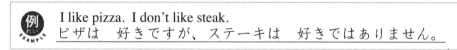

例 I like pizza. I don't like steak.
ピザは　好きですが、ステーキは　好きではありません。

11. I hate swimming. I love skateboarding.

_____

12. I am skilled at playing the guitar. I am not skilled at playing the trumpet (トランペット).

_____

13. I am good at math. I am terrible at English.

_____

14. My friend likes to play cards. I don't like to play cards.

_____

15. My father is excellent at jogging. He is very poor at basketball.

_____

16. My little sister loves cooking. My little brother hates cooking.

_____

17. Atsuko is very skilled at calligraphy (書道). Kenji is not very skilled at calligraphy.

_____

18. My older brother is great at soccer. My older sister is not.

_____

五 Read the following paragraph about Tomoko. Then draw a picture showing Tomoko surrounded by all the things that she is good at and all the things she likes.

友子さんは　私の　友達です。16さいで、高校一年生です。友子さんには　たくさん　好きなことが　あります。テニス部に　いますから、毎日　テニスを　します。友子さんは　漢字を書く事も好きです。学校の科目では数学と　国語が　好きです。でも英語は　あまり　好き　ではありません。時々　生け花も　します。でも　ちょっと　苦手です。音楽も　得意です。ジャズが　好きです。歌うことが　上手　です。毎週カラオケへ　行きます。友子さんんは、ご家族とよく映画を　見に　行きます。それから、友子さんは　ねこが　大好きです。でも、犬は　ちょっと苦手です。

名前：　　　　　　　　　　　　　　　　　　日付：　　　月　　　日

● Practice the *kanji* below tracing the first stroke in the first box, the first and second in the second box, etc. Fill in the other boxes with the complete *kanji*.

色	ノ	ク	ク	名	名	色					
白	ノ	イ	白	白	白						
黒	丶	冂	日	日	甲	甲	里	里	黒	黒	黒
赤	一	十	土	才	亦	赤	赤				
青	一	十	丰	圭	青	青	青	青			

🚹 Write the following phrases using *kanji* and *kana*.

1. The hat is blue.   _____

2. Motoko is good at yoga. (ヨ ガ)   _____

3. I wake up at 5:28 a.m.   _____

4. Emiko likes black.   _____

🚹 Think of visual ways (graphic organizers) you can use to categorize/organize ALL color words from the Chapter 7 New Words list. One possibility might be to list color words that do include the *kanji* 色 in one column, and those that don't in another. Another might be to separate them into groups of warm colors, cool colors, and neutrals. Try to use more than one method to organize the words in the space below.

🈩 Color this picture according to the key below.

5. 白
6. 黒
7. 青
8. 紫
　　むらさき
9. オレンジ
10. 黄色
　　き
11. 赤
12. 緑
　　みどり
13. ピンク

五 Translate each sentence into Japanese using as many *kanji* as possible.

14. I am pretty good at singing, but my older sister is just so-so.

   _____

15. I love (the color) green, but I hate (the color) yellow.

   _____

16. My grandfather is very skilled at golf, but my father is not.

   _____

17. My mother is tall. But my father is short.

   _____

18. That dog is not brown. But that cat is yellow, white, and brown.

   _____

19. I don't eat mochi.

   _____

六 Write the *kanji* stroke order below with the first stroke in the first box, the first and second stroke in the second box, etc. Fill in the full *kanji* in the remaining boxes in each row. In the last row, write another *kanji* from a previous chapter that you feel you need to practice.

色														
白														
黒														
赤														
青														

名前：　　　　　　　　　　　　　　　　　　　　日付：　　　月　　　日

🔊 Listen to the prompts and choose the best responses for the following questions.

Mary is telling her host sister Miho about Mary's family's likes, dislikes, and hobbies.

1. What activity does Mary's family love?
   a. sports
   c. sleeping
   b. eating
   d. anime

2. What is Mary's mother good at?
   a. playing cards and dancing
   c. skiing and mountain climbing
   b. playing cards and singing
   d. skiing and horseback riding

3. How does Miho describe her karate ability?
   a. terrible
   c. she is really good
   b. so so
   d. she has never done karate

4. Mary says her father
   a. doesn't like to cook but is good at it.
   b. likes to cook but is bad at it.
   c. never cooks.
   d. loves to cook and is good at it.

5. Miho and Mary decide to
   a. write a report about their family members' hobbies for school.
   b. make a video of each family member doing their hobby.
   c. teach what they are good at to each other.
   d. stop doing their hobbies for awhile.

名前：　　　　　　　　　　　　　　　　　　日付：　　　月　　　日

➊ Practice the *kanji* below tracing the first stroke in the first box, the first and second in the second box, etc. Fill in the other boxes with the complete *kanji*.

歌	一	亻	亼	哥	哥	可	哥	哥	哥	哥	哥	歌
	歌	歌										
思	丶	冂	冋	用	田	甲	思	思	思			

➋ Write the following using *kanji* and *kana*.

1. Ken likes soba noodles. _____

2. Michiko was born on July 4, 1990. _____

3. The dress is red. _____

4. Hiro is wearing a large kimono. _____

➌ Fill in the blanks with the correct particles と、は、が、の、へ、で、も、に. Use ✕ if no particle is required.

5. たけし君＿＿＿けんたろう君＿＿＿いい　友達です。

6. でも、性格 (personality)＿＿＿　とても　違います。

7. たけし君＿＿＿趣味＿＿＿バスケで、けんたろう君＿＿＿趣味＿＿＿チェス＿＿＿です。

8. たけし君＿＿＿せい＿＿＿高い　ですが、けんたろう君＿＿＿せい＿＿＿とても低い＿＿＿です。

9. たけし君＿＿＿毎日＿＿＿六時＿＿＿起きます。けんたろう君＿＿＿六時半＿＿＿起きて、七時＿＿＿学校＿＿＿行きます。

10. たけし君＿＿＿赤＿＿＿大好き　ですが、けんたろう君＿＿＿黒＿＿＿好きです。

11. たけし君＿＿＿ご家族＿＿＿八人です。けんたろう君＿＿＿ご家族＿＿＿三人です。

12. たけし君＿＿＿よく＿＿＿「僕＿＿＿スーパーマン　です。」＿＿＿言いますが、けんたろう君＿＿＿「僕＿＿＿大学＿＿＿行って、*世界で　一番強い(world's best)＿＿＿チェス・プレーヤーに　なります。」＿＿＿言います。

* 世界 – the world/earth

㈣ Read each sentence carefully, then choose と言いました (...said...) if it is a direct quote, or と思います (I think...) if it is a thought. Next, translate each sentence into English. Model your sentences on the example here.

> 例 幹子さんは、「はい、赤が　好きです。」
> a) と言いました
> b) と思います　　　Mikiko said, "Yes, I like red."

13. 私は　その　靴が　とても　大きい、
   a) と言いました
   b) と思います　＿＿＿＿＿＿＿＿＿＿＿＿＿＿＿＿＿

14. 僕は　*ベガルタ仙台は　いいサッカーのチームだ、
   a) と言いました
   b) と思います　＿＿＿＿＿＿＿＿＿＿＿＿＿＿＿＿＿

15. じゅん君は、「空手が　好きですが、全然　上手では　ありません。」
   a) と言いました
   b) と思います　＿＿＿＿＿＿＿＿＿＿＿＿＿＿＿＿＿

16. アマンダさんは、「その漫画は　長いですね。もう　全部　読みました。」
   a) と言いました
   b) と思います　＿＿＿＿＿＿＿＿＿＿＿＿＿＿＿＿＿

17. 高子さんは、「ここに　鉛筆と　ペンと　紙が　あります。どうぞ、使って下さい。」
   a) と言いました
   b) と思います　＿＿＿＿＿＿＿＿＿＿＿＿＿＿＿＿＿

* ベガルタ仙台 – Begaruta Sendai (soccer team)

五 Translate each sentence into Japanese using as many *kanji* as possible.

18. Bob does not like tofu very much.

_____

19. Sara is not skilled at skiing at all.

_____

20. Mark said, "I am not skilled at skateboarding, and I don't like it at all."

_____

21. I think that this book is very interesting. Please read it.

_____

六 Jumble: The words in the sentences below are out of order. Re-order them to make grammatically-correct sentences in Japanese.

22. ハンバーガー　思います　美味しい　と　は　(I think hamburgers are delicious.)
（お　い）

_____

23. あの　思います　人　だ　は　日本人　と　(I think that person over there is Japanese.)

_____

24. は　と　だ　思います　一年生　静か　(I think that first year students are quiet.)
（しず）

_____

25. 思います　ピザ　まずい　は　と　(I think pizza is terrible.)

_____

七 Writing vertically, write the *kanji* stroke order below with the first stroke in the first box, the first and second stroke in the second box, etc. In the last 2 columns, write other *kanji* that you feel you need to practice.

		花	池	趣	味	事	好	上	色	白	黒	赤	青	歌	思

名前 :　　　　　　　　　　　　　　　日付 :　　　月　　　日

一 Practice the *kanji* below, tracing the first stroke in the first box, the first and second in the second box, etc. Fill in the other boxes with the complete *kanji*.

美	丶	丷	丷	丷	半	羊	关	美	美			
長	丨	厂	匚	匚	镸	長	長	長				
短	ノ	匕	仁	缶	矢	矢	矢	矢	矢	短	短	短
海	丶	冫	氵	氵	沪	汢	海	海	海			

二 Write the following in Japanese using *kanji* and *kana*.

1. June 26, 2009　　　　　　　　　_____

2. My hobby is flower arranging.　_____

3. What color do you like?　　　　_____

4. Please look at this photograph.　_____

三 Translate each phrase into Japanese, making sure the ending for each adjective (い or な) is correct. Use as many 漢字 as possible. Model your sentences on the examples here.

a beautiful hat	美しい　ぼうし
a quiet student	静かな　生徒

5.　a big dog　_____

6.　a strange box　_____

7.　a short pencil　_____

8.　a long beard　_____

9.　a clean ocean　_____

10.　dirty hands　_____

11.　a noisy cat　_____

四 Comment on the photos below. Write at least two sentences for each photo below, including an adjective in each sentence.

例 きれいなしゃしんです。
女の子はかわいいです。

12.　_____

13.　_____

14.　_____

15.　_____

16. _____

17. _____

五 Translate these sentences into Japanese using as many *kanji* as possible.

18. Today is Friday, January 20.

_____

19. It is vacation. I will not go to school.

_____

20. Christy will come to my house by bus. At 12:30, we will eat delicious pizza.

_____

21. Christy is wearing a long skirt. It is very pretty.

_____

22. At 8:30, we will play basketball. It will be fun.

_____

名前：　　　　　　　　　　　　　　　　　日付：　　　月　　　日

● Practice the *kanji* below, tracing the first stroke in the first box, the first and second in the second box, etc. Fill in the other boxes with the complete *kanji*.

安	丶	ヽ	宀	灾	安	安					
悪	一	丆	币	亞	覀	亜	亜	严	悪	悪	悪
面	一	丆	厂	历	而	而	而	面			
天	一	二	天	天							
立	丶	亠	六	立	立						
昔	一	十	廾	共	苗	苗	昔	昔			

		ノ	ケ	々								
々												

Write the following using *kanji* and *kana*.

1. Mr. Suzuki's fingers are short. _____

2. The dog is standing. _____

3. The girl is very beautiful. _____

4. The class is Monday at 2:35 p.m. _____

Fill in the blanks below. The left column is the present tense, and the right column is the past tense. Pay special attention to the differences between い and な adjectives.

Present	**Past**
5. _____	良かったです。
6. 面白いです。 おもしろ	_____
7. _____	悪かったです。
8. _____	元気でした。
9. _____	安かったです。
10. _____	つまらなかったです。
11. きれいです。	_____
12. _____	短かったです。

④ 友さん wrote down what he did yesterday, but he forgot to use the past tense. Change each sentence into the past tense for him, making sure to use the correct past tense ending for い adjectives (〜かったです), な adjectives (〜でした), and for verbs (〜ました or 〜でした).

> 例 おなか が ペコペコ ~~です~~ でした 。 　 おなか が ペコペコ でした。

13. すし を たくさん 食べます。 _____

14. おなか が 大きい です。 _____

15. デパート へ 行きます。 _____

16. 青い パンツ が 好きです。 _____

17. あの デパート の ズボン が 好きです。 _____

18. でも、その パンツ は 高いです。 _____

19. ぼく は ネクタイ が ありません。 _____

20. 緑 の スカート は 買いません。 _____

⑤ Translate these sentences into Japanese using as many 漢字 as possible.

21. On Monday, I went to judo club. _____

22. We practiced from 3:30 until 5:30. _____

23. It was very interesting. _____

24. But, later, my legs and arms hurt. _____

25. At home, I ate dinner and then I took (drank) medicine.

_____

26. At 10:30 p.m., I read a book. It was boring.

_____

27. Then, at 11:45 p.m., I went to sleep.

_____

名前： 日付： 月 日

● Practice the *kanji* below, tracing the first stroke in the first box, the first and second in the second box, etc. Fill in the other boxes with the complete *kanji*.

		一	ナ	才	有	有	有						
有													
広		`	二	广	広	広							
島		'	丨	亻	冂	白	白	鳥	鳥	島	島		

● Write the following using *kanji* and *kana*.

1. Emiko is drinking juice.

    _____

2. My room was clean.

    _____

3. My little sister's birthday is March 23.

    _____

4. Please read that book.

    _____

三 Circle the correct negative tense for each sentence below, according to the English cues. Pay special attention to the い and な adjectives.

5. テレビゲームは_____   Video games are not interesting.
(a) おもしろくないです。   (b) おもしろいではありません。

6. 昨日の 小テストは_____   Yesterday's quiz was not difficult.
(a) 難しくなかったです。   (b) 難しいではありませんでした。

7. 琵琶湖は_____   Lake Biwa is not wide.
(a) 広くないです。   (b) 広いではないです。

8. トム・ハンクスは_____   Tom Hanks is not famous.
(a) 有名くないです。   (b) 有名ではありません。

9. この アップルパイは_____   This apple pie is not delicious.
(a) おいしくないです。   (b) おいしいではないです。

10. 体育の 授業は_____   P.E. class is not difficult.
(a) 難しくありません。   (b) 難しいではないです。

11. その男の人は_____   That man is not handsome.
(a) ハンサムではありません。   (b) ハンサムくないです。

12. あのライオンは_____   That lion over there is not bad.
(a) 悪くないです。   (b) 悪いではありません。

四 Rewrite each of the statements below in the negative and then write the English translation of the new sentence. Model your sentences on the example here.

> 例 今日は 火曜日です。
> EXAMPLE 今日は 火曜日ではありません。 Today is not Tuesday.

13. 今日の 天気は いいですね。

_____

14. 英語の クラスが あります。

_____

15. 日本語の クラスも あります。

_____

16. 日本語の　先生は　怖い　です。
こわ

_____

17. 有名　です。
ゆうめい

_____

18. 宿題は　つまらない　です。
しゅくだい

_____

19. 漢字は　難しいです。
むずか

_____

20. 私の　父は　日本語を　話します。

_____

21. 父と　いっしょに　散歩を　します。
さんぽ

_____

五 Translate each of these sentences into Japanese. Use as many 漢字 as possible.

22. That boy's hair is not very long.

_____

23. But his younger sister's hair is long.

_____

24. His younger sister is a little chubby.

_____

25. Tomokazu likes to play soccer.

_____

26. And, Tomokazu is strong.

_____

27. Tomokazu's younger sister is not strong.

_____

28. But she is good at tennis.

_____

29. The boy and the girl both like sports.

_____

(六) Write the *kanji* stroke order below with the first stroke in the first box, the first and second stroke in the second box, etc. Fill in the remaining boxes with the complete *kanji*.

美														
長														
短														
海														
安														
悪														
面														
天														
立														
昔														
々														

名前：   日付：   月   日

🔊 Listen to the prompts and answer the following questions.

Listen as Mike, an American high school student, and Masa, a Japanese student, discuss American and Japanese high schools in a telephone conference call.

Write the letter for the appropriate answer on the blank.

1. Which high school(s) are big?   _____

2. Which school(s) are small?   _____

3. Which school(s) are famous for sports? _____

4. Which school(s) have a long history?   _____

5. Which school(s) have quiet classes?   _____

6. Which school(s) have delicious lunches? _____

7. Whose teacher is pretty?   _____

a. Masa's only
b. Mike's only
c. BOTH Masa's and Mike's
d. NEITHER Masa's nor Mike's

名前：　　　　　　　　　　　　　　　　　　　　日付：　　　月　　　日

➖ Write the following words using *kanji* and *kana*.

1. Math is not difficult. _____

2. Mariko is studying Japanese. _____

3. English class is at 1:26 p.m. every day. _____

4. All together it is $25. ($ = ドル) _____

⚌ For each short dialogue below, answer each question in the negative. Then translate each ANSWER into English.

> 例 Student A: 先週は　忙しかった　ですか。
> Student B: いいえ、忙しくなかった　です　(*or* 忙しくありませんでした)。
> English: No, last week was not busy.

5. Student A: 夕べの　お寿司は　美味しかった　ですか。

   Student B: _____

   英語: _____

6. Student A: 前の　学校は　大きかった　ですか。

   Student B: _____

   英語: _____

7. Student A: 去年、あなたの　かみの　毛は　長かった　ですか。

   Student B: _____

   英語: _____

8. Student A: 去年の　誕生日パーティーは　楽しかった　ですか。
きょねん　　たんじょうび

   Student B: _____

   英語: _____

9. Student A: 日曜日は　ひま　でしたか。

   Student B: _____

   英語: _____

10. Student A: 月曜日の　小テストの　せいせきは　悪かった　ですか。

   Student B: _____

   英語: _____

11. Student A: あの　絵は　美しかった　ですか。
え

   Student B: _____

   英語: _____

12. Student A: 水泳の　後、足と　手は　痛かった　ですか。
すいえい　　あと　　　　　　　　　いた

   Student B: _____

   英語: _____

13. Student A: その本は　面白かった　ですか。

   Student B: _____

   英語: _____

名前：   日付：   月   日

➖ Write the following in Japanese using *kanji* and *kana*.

1. Our high school baseball team was not strong._____

2. That cat is not beautiful.   _____

3. Kentarou is swimming.   _____

4. I studied at home yesterday.   _____

🟰 Complete the chart below. Make sure you know whether you are working with an い adjective or a な adjective. Try to finish without looking at your textbook. Note: Write at least one answer on each blank, though there may be more than one possible answer.

Adjective (non-past tense)	い adj. or な adj.	Past tense 〜かったです or でした	Negative 〜くありません / 〜くないです or 〜ではありません / 〜ではないです (or じゃ in place of では)	Negative past 〜くありませんでした / 〜くなかったです or 〜ではありませんでした / 〜ではなかったです(or じゃ in place of では)	英語
いそがしい	5.	6.	7.	8.	9.
10.	11.	おいしかったです。	12.	13.	14.
15.	16.	17.	18.	うるさくなかったです。	19.
20.	21.	22.	23.	24.	cute
25.	26.	27.	きれいではありません	28.	29.
こわい	30.	31.	32.	33.	34.
35.	36.	37.	38.	39.	famous
40.	41.	つまらなかったです。	42.	43.	44.

三 Complete the writing below according to the English cues.

きのう、(45)＿＿＿＿＿＿＿＿(kindergarten)の　友達に　会いました。ひさしぶり
でした。友だちの　(46)＿＿＿＿＿＿＿＿(name)は　あやこちゃんです。六さいの
とき、あやこちゃんは　せいが　(47)＿＿＿＿＿＿＿(a little)　(48)＿＿＿＿＿＿＿
(was short)です。でも、今は、せいが　(49)＿＿＿＿＿＿＿(is tall)です。それに、
六さいの　とき、あやこちゃんの　髪の　毛は(50)＿＿＿＿＿＿＿(was long)です。
でも、今は、髪の　毛は　(51)＿＿＿＿＿＿＿(is not long)です。六さいのとき、
あやこちゃんと　いっしょに　良く　けんか*を　しました。でも、今は、
(52)＿＿＿＿＿＿＿(good)友達です。それと、六さいの　とき、あやこちゃんは
頭が　(53)＿＿＿＿＿＿＿(was good)です。そして、今も　頭が(54)＿＿＿＿＿＿＿(very)
いいです！
あたま

*けんかをする：to argue

四 Use the cues below to make complete sentences in Japanese. Add additional words and particles as
needed.

> 例　きれい　人　たくさん　　　affirmative present
> れい
> EXAMPLE　この教室に　たくさんの　きれいな　人が　います。
> There are a lot of pretty people in this classroom.

55. 忙しい　　　　弟　　　　いつも　　　　affirmative present
いそが

＿＿＿＿＿＿＿＿＿＿＿＿＿＿＿＿＿＿＿＿＿＿＿＿＿＿＿＿＿＿＿＿＿

The younger brother is always busy.

56. 着物　　　　安い　　　　あきこさん　　　negative past
き

＿＿＿＿＿＿＿＿＿＿＿＿＿＿＿＿＿＿＿＿＿＿＿＿＿＿＿＿＿＿＿＿＿

Akiko's kimono was not cheap.

57. 有名　　　　先生　　　　ちょっと　　　affirmative past
ゆうめい

＿＿＿＿＿＿＿＿＿＿＿＿＿＿＿＿＿＿＿＿＿＿＿＿＿＿＿＿＿＿＿＿＿

The teacher was a little famous.

58. 花　　　　高い　　　　ベンさん　　　negative past

＿＿＿＿＿＿＿＿＿＿＿＿＿＿＿＿＿＿＿＿＿＿＿＿＿＿＿＿＿＿＿＿＿

Ben's flowers were not expensive.

59. 広い 　　　　　海 　　　　　　　　　affirmative present

_____

The ocean is wide.

60. 手 　　　　小さい 　　　　　妹 　　　　　affirmative past

_____

My younger sister's hands are small.

61. (free choice sentence using the negative past of an adjective)

_____

英語： _____

五 Write the *kanji* stroke order below with the first stroke in the first box, the first and second stroke in the second box, etc. In any remaining boxes, write the full *kanji*.

島													
長													
短													
海													
広													
悪													
面													
天													
立													
昔													

名前：　　　　　　　　　　　　　　　　日付：　　　月　　　日

🔊 Listen to the prompts and choose the best responses for the following questions.

Junko and Masayo, two teachers, discuss what they did over their winter vacation. Junko went to Hawaii and Masayo went to Hokkaidō.

Write the letter of the appropriate answer on the blank.

1. Which of the two said the ocean was very beautiful?　____

2. Which of the two talked about eating ramen and potatoes?　____

3. Which of the two said the beach was long?　____

4. Which of the two said that everyone was kind?　____

5. Which of the two said the food was delicious?　____

6. Which of the two said the shopping was very fun?　____

7. Which of the two said they were a little busy?　____

a. only Junko
b. only Masayo
c. BOTH Junko and Masayo
d. NEITHER Junko nor Masayo

名前：   日付：   月   日

❶ Practice the *kanji* below, tracing the first stroke in the first box, the first and second in the second box, etc. Fill in the other boxes with the complete *kanji*.

買	丶	冂	冂	罒	罒	罒	罒	胃	買	買	買
売	一	十	士	声	声	声	売				
店	丶	亠	广	广	庁	庁	店	店			
万	一	丁	万								

❷ Write the following words using *kanji* and *kana*. (Yen [¥] = 円 [えん])

1. Masumi loves (the color) blue. _____

2. The party is from 7:54 p.m. _____

3. We went shopping in Shibuya. _____

4. The shoes were ¥12,000. _____

三 Read each of these numbers out loud, in Japanese, and then write each out in *kanji* and *kana*. Remember, 一万 = 10,000. Model your sentences on the example here.
　　まん

> **例** ¥13,500　　一万三千五百円
> いちまんさんぜんごひゃくえん

5.　¥21,200　_____

6.　¥8,900　_____

7.　¥55,600　_____

8.　¥47,100　_____

9.　¥18,350　_____

10.　¥6,225　_____

11.　¥94,431　_____

四 Write each phrase in Japanese, using the appropriate noun plus dictionary form verb. Use as many 漢字 as possible. Model your sentences on the example here.

> **例** to fight　　けんかを　する

12.　to study　_____

13.　to go shopping　_____

14.　to take a walk　_____

15.　to take a trip　_____

五 Jumble: The words in the sentences below are out of order. Re-order them to make grammatically-correct sentences in Japanese.

16.　食事　しました　友さん　を　は　に　八時　(Tomo had a meal at 8:00.)

_____

17.　レポート　タイプ　を　昨日　私　しました　は　(I typed the report yesterday.)
　　　　　　　　　　　きのう

_____

18. 数学 良和さん しました 勉強 は を (Yoshikazu studied math.)

_____

19. 下さい に お母さん 電話 を して (Please telephone your mother.)

_____

20. は 兄 を 見ました 映画 に 土曜日
(My older brother watched a movie on Saturday.)

_____

六 Translate each of the following into Japanese using the appropriate noun plus dictionary form verb, and as many 漢字 as possible.

例 EXAMPLE	to play basketball	バスケを する

21. to go on a date _____

22. to (sing) karaoke _____

23. to shower _____

24. to do homework _____

名前：	日付： 　　月 　　日

➖➊ Write a short (at least 4 lines) paragraph about your activities last week. Remember to use the PAST tense of the verb. Use transition words like それから、そして、 or それに to connect your sentences. For instance, if you went on a date on Saturday, you might say:

土曜日の晩、友達と　デートを　しました。それから・・・・

_____

_____

_____

_____

_____

_____

➖➋ Insert quotation marks where appropriate in the paragraphs below.

先生は、えんぴつで　書いて下さいと　言いました。すると、じゅん君は、

先生、僕は　えんぴつが　ありませんと　言いました。すると、明子さんは、

じゅん君、このえんぴつを　どうぞと　言いました。

➖➌ Translate these sentences into Japanese using as many 漢字 as possible.

1. Yesterday was Saturday, March 24.

_____

2. I went shopping with my friend. I bought two blue T-shirts.

_____

3. In the afternoon, I walked the dog. And then, I did some science homework.

_____

4. The homework was very difficult. I studied from 4 p.m. until 6:30 p.m.

    _____

5. For dinner, we had a meal at a Chinese restaurant. The food was delicious. I love to eat Chinese food.

    _____

㊃ Write the *kanji* stroke order below with the first stroke in the first box, the first and second stroke in the second box, etc. Fill in the remaining boxes in that row with the same *kanji*. Use the last row to write *kanji* that you feel you need to practice.

買														
売														
店														
万														

名前：　　　　　　　　　　　　　　　　　　　　日付：　　　月　　　日

● Practice the *kanji* below, tracing the first stroke in the first box, the first and second in the second box, etc. Fill in the other boxes with the complete *kanji*.

全	ノ	八	仝	仐	仐	全					
部	゛	亠	产	产	立	产	音	音	音⁷	部⁷	部
円	I	冂	冂	円							

● Write the following words using *kanji* and *kana*.

1. Mr. Yamazaki sells books.　　　_____

2. Mom went to Japan in 2008.　　_____

3. Tonight I will do homework.　　_____

4. Please take a shower before dinner.　_____

三 Write the correct number of objects/things with the most appropriate counter.

5. _____ 6. _____ 7. _____

8. _____ 9. _____ 10. _____

11. _____ 12. _____ 13. _____

四 Translate these sentences into 日本語. Be careful to use the correct counter.

14. Please give me 10 ballpoint pens.

_____

15. At my house, I have three dogs and two cats.

_____

16. For breakfast, I drank two cups of green tea.

_____

17. Yesterday I bought four books at the bookstore.

_____

㊄ Jenny is going shopping for school supplies with her friend Kenji. Help her by filling in the blanks with useful shopping expressions. Then answer questions 23-25 in English.

18. けんじ　：　_____。(Excuse me!)

19. 店員　　：　_____。(Welcome!)

　　けんじ　：このノートは_____(how much)ですか。

20. 店員　　：それですか。_____(five)で　_____(900 yen)です。

21. ジェニー：ちょっと_____(expensive)ですね。その_____(eraser)
　　　　　　は　_____(how much)ですか。

　　店員　　：消しゴムですか。消しゴムは　一つ、50円です。

22. ジェニー：いいですね。消しゴムを　三つと　えんぴつを　_____(six)
　　　　　　下さい。じゃ、1000円から、お願いします。

　　店員　　：1000円　おあずかりします。はい、250円の　おかえしでございま
　　　　　　す。ありがとうございました。また、どうぞ。

23. What sort of store are Kenji and Jenny going to?

_____

24. What did Jenny buy?

_____

25. How much were Jenny's purchases?

_____

名前：   日付：   月   日

➊ Practice the *kanji* below, tracing the first stroke in the first box, the first and second in the second box, etc. Fill in the other boxes with the complete *kanji*.

暗	丨	冂	冃	日	日`	日亠	日立	日产	晬	暗	暗	暗
	暗											

明	丨	冂	冃	日	日J	明	明	明				

➋ Write the following using *kanji* and *kana*.

1. That movie is not interesting. _____

2. Please give me a taller one. _____

3. The total is 500 yen. _____

4. That jacket is 56,792 yen. _____

➌ Translate each sentence below into 日本語. Model your sentences on the example below.

> 例 Do you have a larger size? <u>もっと　大きいサイズは　ありますか。</u>

5. Do you have smaller computer? _____

6. Do you have a cuter T-shirt? _____

7. Do you have a more delicious cake? _____

8. Do you have a more expensive bag? _____

9. Do you have a more interesting class? _____

10. Do you have a brighter room? _____

11. Do you have a scarier movie? _____

四 You and your Japanese friend さわこ are spending the day in an upscale residential and shopping area of 東京. You thought the two of you were just going window shopping, but さわこ has other ideas. Fill in the blanks in the dialogue below with the correct 日本語、 using the English cues. For the last two lines of dialogue, add your own ending. Then answer in English the questions that follow.

(*on the street*)

You　　：　あの高いビルは (12) ＿＿＿＿＿＿＿＿＿＿＿＿ (what) ですか。

さわこ：　あれは　六本木ヒルズです。(13) ＿＿＿＿＿＿＿＿＿ (taller one) も　ありますよ。あそこを見てください。さあ、(14)＿＿＿＿＿＿＿＿＿。 (let's go)

(*inside the shopping center*)

さわこ：　あの店、いいですね。私は　(15) ＿＿＿＿＿＿＿＿＿＿＿ (new) くつを 買います。

(*to the clerk*) もっと大きいのは　ありますか。

店員　　：　はい、ちょっと待って下さい。

You　　：　さわこさん、この　ハイヒールは　好き　ですか。

さわこ：　ええ、(16)＿＿＿＿＿＿ (love)です。でも、(17)＿＿＿＿＿ (cheaper ones) が　いい　です。

店員　　：　これは　どうですか。こちらは　一万円です。

さわこ：　ええと、この(18) ＿＿＿＿＿＿ (color)は　あまり　好きじゃない　です。
(19)＿＿＿＿＿＿ (a blue one) は　ありますか。

20. You　　：　＿＿＿＿＿＿＿＿＿＿＿＿＿＿＿＿＿＿＿＿＿＿＿＿＿＿＿＿＿＿

21. さわこ：　＿＿＿＿＿＿＿＿＿＿＿＿＿＿＿＿＿＿＿＿＿＿＿＿＿＿＿＿＿＿

22. The two girls are going to what part of Tokyo?

＿＿＿＿＿＿＿＿＿＿＿＿＿＿＿＿＿＿＿＿＿＿＿＿＿＿＿＿＿＿＿＿＿＿＿＿＿＿＿

23. What does Sawako want to buy?

＿＿＿＿＿＿＿＿＿＿＿＿＿＿＿＿＿＿＿＿＿＿＿＿＿＿＿＿＿＿＿＿＿＿＿＿＿＿＿

24. What is the yen cost of the object the clerk brings?

＿＿＿＿＿＿＿＿＿＿＿＿＿＿＿＿＿＿＿＿＿＿＿＿＿＿＿＿＿＿＿＿＿＿＿＿＿＿＿

25. What was wrong with the first object Sawako looked at? What was wrong with the second object?

_____

_____

26. Do you have any friends like Sawako? If so, what personality traits do you think your friend and Sawako have in common?

_____

_____

五 Translate these sentences into English.

27. 私は　今日、ペットを　買います。あなたも　ペットストアーへ　行きません か。

_____

28. 私は、かめが　好き　です。かわいいのを　見せて下さい。

_____

29. そのかめは　色が　ちょっと暗い　ですね。もっと明るい　色の　かめは　いま すか。

_____

30. ああ、この亀は　美しい　です。これを　下さい。いくら　ですか。

_____

31. 一万三千円　です。はい、一万五千円　お預かりします (to gather, receive)。

_____

32. いいですね。この亀の　名前は、「亀」です。静かな　友達　です。

_____

名前： 日付： 月 日

🔊 Listen to the prompts and choose the best responses for the following questions.

Lisa is Canadian. Soon after moving in with her home-stay family in Japan, she realizes she has neglected to bring a gift for her host mother. She goes to an import store in Tokyo called National Azabu, to try to buy something from her home country to give her.

1. Lisa asks for a _____.
   a. cheaper one   b. better brand
   c. smaller one   d. larger one

2. What is Lisa doing in Japan?
   a. working   b. sightseeing
   c. studying   d. missionary work

3. How much does a small bottle cost?

   _____

4. How much money does Lisa give to the store clerk?

   _____

5. How much change does she get back?

   _____

名前：	日付：	月	日

● Write the following using *kanji* and *kana*.

1. Welcome! (to a store customer) _____

2. At 5 p.m., the art classroom was dark. _____

3. My dog does not like tofu very much. _____

4. Takako bought five new pencils. _____

● It's Hanako's birthday, and Mari has come to give her a present. Later, their friend Tomohiro joins them. Read the dialogue below and fill in the blanks with the correct word or particle.

まり：　花子さん、誕生日おめでとう。この　プレゼントを　どうぞ。

花子：　あ、どうもありがとう。(5. I receive)_____。

まり：　それは　何　ですか。プレゼント　です(6. question particle)_____?

花子：　はい、家族 (7. from)_____の　プレゼント　です。母 (8. from)_____この　ステキな　ネックレスを　(9. received)_____。そして、私は漫画を　三 (10. volumes, books)_____　(11. received)_____。

まり：　いいですね。私の　プレゼントを　(12. please open)_____。

花子：　わあ、美味しそうですね。これは　どこの　おせんべいですか。

まり：　京都の　おせんべい　です。食べて見て下さい。

友弘：　花子さん、誕生日おめでとう。

花子：　あ、友弘さん、ありがとう。このおせんべいを　いっしょに　食べませんか。まりさん (13. from)_____　(14. received)_____。

友弘：　(15. I humbly receive)_____。美味しいですねえ。でも、スペインの　せんべいは (16. more)_____美味しいですよ！

花子とまり：　へええ！

三 It is the day after your mother's birthday. You are talking on the phone to your friend and telling him about the presents your mother received from you, and other family members. Make up and write a short story (at least 6 lines) about the gifts your mother received, using the appropriate verbs of giving and receiving. For instance, if your father gave your mother a watch, you might write:

父は　母に　すばらしい時計を　あげました。

_____

_____

_____

_____

_____

_____

四 Translate each sentence into Japanese using the appropriate verb tense and as many 漢字 as possible. Model your sentences on the example below.

> **例** Yesterday, I argued with my friend Mayumi.
> **EXAMPLE** 昨日、友達の　まゆみさんと　けんかを　しました。

17. Today, we made up.

_____

18. This morning, I received a new notebook from Mayumi.

_____

19. This afternoon, I received five flowers from Mayumi. I don't like flowers very much.

_____

20. So then, I gave the flowers back to Mayumi. And I gave her a lucky charm (おまもり).

_____

21. This evening, we went shopping together, and bought two large-size red T-shirts.

_____

22. Tomorrow, I will wear one red T-shirt. Mayumi will also wear one red T-shirt.

_____

23. I like Mayumi a lot!

_____

🈝 Review your kanji charts for the lessons you have completed so far. In the space below, practice writing previously learned *kanji* that you feel you need to practice. Try to write each of those *kanji* at least 5 times, saying them out loud as you write them.

名前：＿＿＿＿＿＿＿＿＿＿＿＿＿＿＿＿＿＿ 日付： 月 日

⊖ Write the following words using *kanji* and *kana*.

1. Kentaro has long hair. ＿＿＿＿＿＿＿＿＿＿＿＿＿＿＿＿＿＿＿

2. His father's shoes were ¥17,100. ＿＿＿＿＿＿＿＿＿＿＿＿＿＿＿＿＿＿＿

3. The Japanese room (和室) is a bright (light) room. ＿＿＿＿＿＿＿＿＿＿＿＿＿

4. My friend is doing his homework. ＿＿＿＿＿＿＿＿＿＿＿＿＿＿＿＿＿＿＿

⊜ Fill in the blanks with the correct particle. Use ✕ if no particle is needed.

きのう (5)＿＿＿＿＿＿ 兄 (6)＿＿＿＿＿＿ １９才 (7)＿＿＿＿＿＿ 誕生日でした。

おじいさん (8)＿＿＿＿＿＿ 兄 (9)＿＿＿＿＿＿ お金 (10)＿＿＿＿＿＿ あげました。

僕 (11)＿＿＿＿＿＿ 兄 (12)＿＿＿＿＿＿ 面白い ＤＶＤ (13)＿＿＿＿＿＿ あげました。

兄 (14)＿＿＿＿＿＿ 父 (15)＿＿＿＿＿＿ 母 (16)＿＿＿＿＿＿ 黒いくつ (17)＿＿＿＿＿＿

もらいました。

兄 (18)＿＿＿＿＿＿ 犬 (19)＿＿＿＿＿＿ ねこ (20)＿＿＿＿＿＿ 鳥 (bird) (21)＿＿＿＿＿＿ あまり 好

きではありません。

でも、 かめ (22)＿＿＿＿＿＿ 大好きです。 毎日 (23)＿＿＿＿＿＿ かめ (24)＿＿＿＿＿＿ お水

(25)＿＿＿＿＿＿ やります。

きのう (26)＿＿＿＿＿＿ 、 おじいさん (27)＿＿＿＿＿＿ 僕 (28)＿＿＿＿＿＿ 二万円

(29)＿＿＿＿＿＿ くれました。 僕 (30)＿＿＿＿＿＿ 誕生日ではありませんでした

(31)＿＿＿＿＿＿ 、 僕 (32)＿＿＿＿＿＿ うれしかったです。 おじいさん、 ありがとう！

⊜ Translate each sentence on the following page into Japanese using the appropriate verb tense. Use as many 漢字 as possible. Model your sentences on the example below.

 例 Last week, my friend gave my little sister two CDs.
先週、 私の 友達は 妹に ＣＤを 二枚 くれました。

33. My uncle gave my mother seven beautiful flowers and two books.

_____

34. My mother gave one flower to my little sister.

_____

35. Tom and Mike played video games on Saturday from 1 p.m. until 4 p.m.

_____

36. Tom is very good at playing video games. He received a good prize (賞).
しょう

_____

37. Mike gave me a fun video game. I like playing video games, but I am not very skilled at them.

_____

38. The teacher also loves playing video games. He sometimes plays games after school.

_____

39. Next weekend, we will all play video games together. I think we will all receive prizes!

_____

四 Draw a picture of yourself, or someone in your family, receiving at least three presents. Then write a paragraph, in Japanese, describing who gave what to whom.

名前 :

日付 : 　　月　　日

🔊 Listen to the prompts and choose the best responses for the following questions.

Akiko is going to give her friend Nanami a birthday present and talk about what else Nanami got for her birthday.

1. Nanami thought her present from Akiko was:
    a. big
    c. interesting
    b. expensive
    d. cute

2. Akiko gave Nanami _____.
    a. chocolate
    c. a necklace
    b. money
    d. a stuffed animal

3. Nanami received money and _____ from her father.

4. What did Nanami get from her mother? _____

5. Who gave Nanami three roses? _____

名前：   日付：   月   日

➊ Practice the *kanji* below, tracing the first stroke in the first box, the first and second in the second box, etc. Fill in the other boxes with the complete *kanji*.

春	一	二	三	丰	夫	表	春	春	春		
夏	一	丆	厂	丏	百	百	百	頁	夏	夏	
秋	丿	二	千	千	禾	禾	利	秒	秋		
冬	丿	勹	夂	冬	冬						
石	一	丆	丆	石	石						

二 Translate the following sentences using *kanji* and *kana*.

1. My friend's house is very bright.

   _____

2. These white shoes are a little dirty.

   _____

3. The ryokan in Nara is ¥37,500.

   _____

4. I will go to Miyajima with my Japanese teacher for summer vacation.

   _____

三 Read these clues to determine which season is being described and write the answer (in Japanese) on the blank at the right. Then answer the question at the bottom for each in Japanese.

5. スキーを　します。
   クリスマスの　プレゼントを　もらいます。
   雪だるまを　作ります。
   暖かい　飲み物が　おいしい　です。
   　　　　　　　どの　季節ですか。　　_____

6. 泳ぎます。
   外で　よく　ピクニックを　します。
   *スイカが　美味しいです。
   アイスクリームを　時々　食べます。
   　　　　　　　どの　季節ですか。　　_____

7. アメリカで　学校が　はじまります。
   *りんごが　美味しいです。
   あまり　暑くないです。
   セーターを　時々　着ます。
   　　　　　　　どの　季節ですか。　　_____

8. 桜が　きれいです。
   小鳥も　たくさん　います。
   風が　強いです。
   野球を　します。
   日本で　学校が　はじまります
   　　　　　　　どの　季節ですか。　　_____

*すいか - watermelon; りんご - apple

9. あなたは　どの　季節が　一番　好き　ですか。　なぜ　ですか。
いちばん

_____

_____

_____

㊃ Put each weather-related phrase into Japanese using as many 漢字 as possible. The first one is done for you.

例	明日は、雨が　降るでしょう。 Tomorrow it will probably rain.

10. _____ It is raining now.

11. _____ Today is very hot.

12. _____ Tomorrow will be cooler (more cool).

13. _____ It will be windy (the wind is strong).

14. _____ Yesterday there was a large rainfall.

15. _____ There will probably be snow tomorrow.

16. _____ Friday will be clear (nice).

17. _____ There will be a typhoon in August.

㊄ Use a newspaper, TV, or online report to find a weather report for your city. Write out a short (at least 5 lines) weather report for today and a weather forecast for tomorrow in Japanese.

_____

_____

_____

_____

_____

_____

_____

名前：   日付：   月   日

● Practice the *kanji* below, tracing the first stroke in the first box, the first and second in the second box, etc. Fill in the other boxes with the complete *kanji*.

使	ノ	イ	仁	仁	仨	佢	使	使				
作	ノ	イ	仁	亡	作	作	作					

● Translate the following sentences using *kanji* and *kana*.

1. It is 32 degrees in Akita now.   _____

2. Tomorrow it will probably snow.   _____

3. My little brother received ¥10,000.   _____

4. How much does this manga cost?   _____

● Use the English cues to politely invite your Japanese friend to do each activity with you.

 go camping during summer vacation in Colorado
夏休みに　コロラドで　キャンプを　しませんか。

5. play football on Saturday at 11 a.m.

_____

6. go skiing in Germany during winter break

_____

7. study Japanese at my house on Sunday

_____

8. come to my birthday party next month

_____

9. go to a rock concert next week

_____

10. see a movie Friday night

_____

11. go swimming Wednesday at 6:30 p.m.

_____

12. dine with my family at a Chinese restaurant

_____

四 Fill in the blanks with the correct Japanese word according to the English cue. Be careful to use the correct form of the verb. Then answer the comprehension questions at the end of the dialogue.

慶子 ： ねえ、隆君、ケーキを (13. shall we make) _____ ？
けいこ

隆 ： ええと、(14. cooking) _____は
たかし
(15. a little)_____ ・・・・

慶子 ： そう ですか。実は、きのう、卵を (16. a lot) _____
けいこ   じつ   たまご
もらいましたが、家族は (17. nobody)_____卵を 食べま
ぞく
せん。(18. it's too bad)_____。じゃあ、オムレツはどう
ですか。卵を たくさん (19. use)_____。
たまご

隆 ： ええと、僕は オムレツも ちょっと・・・・
たかし   ぼく

慶子 ： 卵を 使う 料理は、(20. nothing)_____食べませんね。
けいこ たまご つか りょうり
じゃ、映画は どう ですか。
えいが

隆 ： いいですね。映画を (21. let's see) _____ ！
たかし   えいが

22. What two things does Takashi NOT like? _____

23. What does Keiko have a lot of? _____

24. What do the two of them finally decide to do? _____

名前：

日付：　　月　　日

🔊 Listen to the prompts and choose the best responses for the following questions.

1. What is the weather forecast for Saturday?
    a. sunny   b. rainy
    c. cloudy   d. hot

2. What will the weather probably be on Sunday?
    a. sunny   b. rainy
    c. cloudy   d. cold

3. Sunday's weather will be _____.
    a. cold   b. hot
    c. windy   d. rainy

4. Where will they go?
    a. dancing   b. bowling
    c. to sing karaoke   d. to see a movie

➖ Translate the following sentences using *kanji* and *kana*.

1. Write your essay on the computer.   _____

2. Shall we see a movie?   _____

3. Would you like to make yakisoba with me? _____

4. Kenji will not go anywhere this summer.   _____

➕ Pretend you are the people in the following pictures and write down what you want to do in Japanese using the 〜たい form of the verb.

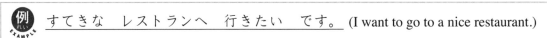
例 <u>すてきな　レストランへ　行きたい　です。</u> (I want to go to a nice restaurant.)

（バスケ）   5. _____

（ボウリング）   6. _____

（食事）   7. _____

（カラオケ）   8. _____

（デート）

9. _____

（さんぽ）

10. _____

（ギター / ひきます）

11. _____

（まんが/ 読みます）

12. _____

Pick ten verbs from the word bank on the following page to make complete sentences, using one of the verbs you have chosen in the designated tense and time phrase. You may need to add other details to create a good sentence.

例 あした ～ましょう → あした、友達と あそびましょう。

13. きのう ～ませんでした _____

14. 来週 ～でしょう _____

15. 今日 ～ませんか _____

16. 今朝（けさ） ～ました _____

17. 今晩（こんばん） ～でしょうか _____

18. おととい ～ませんでした _____

19. 十二月 ～ます

20. 金曜日　～たい _____

21. 来年　～たい _____

22. 先月　～ました _____

作ります	使います	遊びます	晴れます
降ります	します	買います	売ります
いただきます	上げます	もらいます	くれます
やります	探します	旅行します	書きます

㊃ Write the *kanji* stroke order below with the first stroke in the first box, the first and second stroke in the second box, etc. In the last row, write another *kanji* from a previous chapter that you feel you need to practice.

春												
夏												
秋												
冬												
石												

名前 :   日付 :   月   日

➖ Practice the *kanji* below, tracing the first stroke in the first box, the first and second in the second box, etc. Fill in the other boxes with the complete *kanji*.

当	丷	丷	丷	当	当	当						

➋ Translate the following sentences using *kanji* and *kana*.

1. My mother is very smart.

   _____

2. There will probably be heavy rain in Sendai tomorrow.

   _____

3. There is a very big stone in the garden.

   _____

4. Shun likes to eat sushi.

   _____

➌ You are feeling contrary. Your friend is talking about things that you don't want to do or that didn't happen to you. Use the negative form of the verbs he uses to tell him that you don't want to do these things, or that they didn't happen to you. Then translate your negative sentence into English. Be careful to distinguish verb tenses. Model your sentences on the example below.

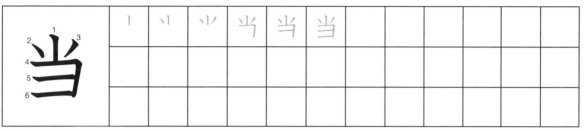

友達：	私は　煎餅が　食べたい　です。
You：	私は、煎餅は　食べたくありません。
	or 私は、煎餅は　食べたくない　です。
	I do not want to eat senbei.

5. 私は、テニスラケットを　父に　もらいました。

_____

_____

6. 私は、昨日、ピクニックに　行きました。
　　　　きのう

_____

_____

7. 私は、映画を　見たかった　です。
　　　えいが

_____

_____

8. 私は、テニスが　大好き　です。

_____

_____

9. 昨日　は　晴れ　でした。
　　　　　は

_____

_____

10. 私は、プロの　テニスプレイヤーに　会いたい　です。
　　　　　　　　　　　　　　　　　あ

_____

_____

11. 私は、毎日、テニスを　したい　です。

_____

_____

12. 明日 学校へ　行きたいです。
　　あした

_____

_____

四 Draw a picture of yourself in the center of the space below. On the left side, draw 4 things you have already received from someone. On the right side, draw 4 things you have not yet received but will. Then write a paragraph, in Japanese, 1. describing what you received, adding information about from whom you received it; 2. describing what you've not yet received; and 3. details about two things you want to receive and from whom.

_____

_____

_____

_____

五 Write the *kanji* stroke order below with the first stroke in the first box, the first and second stroke in the second box, etc. (You might have leftover boxes after you have completely written the *kanji* but go ahead and fill in the remaining boxes in that row with the same *kanji*.) Then fill in the remaining rows with other *kanji* that you feel you need to practice.

当														
作														
使														

名前：　　　　　　　　　　　　　　　　　日付：　　月　　日

● Practice the *kanji* below, tracing the first stroke in the first box, the first and second in the second box, etc. Fill in the other boxes with the complete *kanji*.

桜	一	十	才	术	术	术	术	栌	栌	桜		

● Translate the following sentences using *kanji* and *kana*.

1. I want to drink water. _____

2. It was windy in Sapporo. _____

3. My hobby is drawing pictures. _____

4. August was hot in Kansai. _____

● Translate these sentences into Japanese using the verb pattern in parentheses and as many *kanji* as possible.

5. I like to travel.

_____（すること）

6. I want to go to Japan in June.

_____（～たい）

7. I like summer a lot.

_____（いちばん）

8. I want to see Kyoto in the spring.

_____（～たい）

9. In October the trees will probably be beautiful.

_____（でしょう）

10. There are many temples in Kyoto.

_____ （あります）

11. I want to eat chocolate ice cream（チョコレートアイスクリーム）.

_____ （～たい）

12. In fall, it probably rains sometimes.

_____ （でしょう）

13. I will take a backpack.

_____ （もっていく）

14. I want to buy presents, and give them to my family.

_____ （～て/～たい）

15. Japan should be fun!

_____ （でしょう）

四 You have been invited to both of the following events, A and B. You really want to attend both, but you are not quite sure whether they conflict or not since you probably are not able to read all of the information. To help you solve your dilemma, answer the questions below, in English or in Japanese after reviewing both invitations. Then, once you have determined whether you can attend or not, write out your schedule for that day (use Japanese) to show your Japanese friends.

A.

お花見をしませんか。
日時：四月五日土曜日
　　　　午後一時から午後九時半まで
場所：上野公園しのばずの池
　　　　うえのこうえん
その他：食べ物を持って来て下さい。
連絡先：四月一日までにキアラの携帯
(03-2XXX-9XXX) に連絡をして下さい。

B.

```
大セール中
木村デパート銀座店
住所：東京都中央区日本橋 2－4－1
電話：03-2XXX-9XXX
出口：地下鉄銀座線、 日本橋駅 B 1
四月五日だけ！
午前八時半から午後九時まで
```

16. What are the two events you are invited to attend?

_____

17. What time does each begin? What time does each end?

_____

18. Where does each event take place?

_____

19. Will you be able to attend both? If yes, describe how. If no, tell why not.

_____

_____

_____

_____

20. What do you think you would do at each event?

_____

21. Which event would you look forward to more? Why?

_____

_____

_____

_____

五 Use 日本語 to write out your schedule for tomorrow based upon the previous invitations. Be as detailed as you can (include times, places, and people) and use as many *kanji* as you can. Write a minimum of 5 sentences.

_____

_____

_____

_____

_____

_____

_____

_____

_____

六 Write the *kanji* stroke order below with the first stroke in the first box, the first and second stroke in the second box, etc. Fill in the remaining boxes with the full *kanji*. Use the remaining rows to practice other *kanji* you have found to be difficult to remember.

桜														

名前：　　　　　　　　　　　　　　　　　　　　日付：　　　月　　　日

🔊 Listen to the prompts and choose the best responses for the following questions.

1-4. Number these in order, to indicate the order in which they occur in the listening selection.

_____ Karaoke

_____ Dance

_____ See a movie

_____ Swim

5. What does the girl want to do?
   a. shop   b. travel
   c. homework   d. read a book

6. What else does the girl say she wants to do?
   a. know the boy better   b. say goodbye
   c. call the police   d. meet a friend

名前：   日付：   月   日

➊ Translate the following sentences using *kanji* and *kana*.

1. Please lend me one thousand yen. _____

2. Masumi is eating tenpura with (by means of) chopsticks.

    _____

3. The movie is from 8:20 until 10:35. _____

4. I want to drink coffee and green tea. _____

➋ Fill in each blank with the correct particle. Use ✕ if no particle is required.

5. 私_____名前_____アマンダです。

6. 毎日_____六時四十五分_____おきて、それから、朝ご飯_____食べて、
    学校_____行きます。

7. 学校_____カフェテリア_____友達_____昼ご飯_____食べます。

8. 三時_____四時半_____図書館_____レポート_____書きます。

9. レポート_____コンピューター_____タイプ_____します。

10. 土曜日_____よく_____買い物_____します。

11. 友達_____いっしょ_____デパート_____行きます。

12. 私_____Ｔ－シャツ_____たくさん_____持っていますが、もっと
    _____買いたいです。

13. 私_____先週_____土曜日_____赤い_____Ｔ－シャツ_____二枚
    買いました。

14. それから、パン屋_____ドーナツ_____パン_____カップケーキを　買っ
    て、家_____帰りました。先週の土曜日はたのしい一日でした！

Fill in each blank with the correct counter. In cases where you can write the kanji, also put in the *furigana*. Then put each sentence into English. Model your sentences on the example below.

> 例 机 の 上 に　水 が 三本　ありました。
> （つくえ）（れい）
> EXAMPLE There were three bottles of water on the desk.

15. あの庭の中に花が二十＿＿＿＿＿＿＿あります。きれいですね。
（にわ）

_____

_____

16. 紙を三＿＿＿＿＿＿＿下さい。
（かみ）

_____

_____

17. それから、ボールペン七＿＿＿＿＿＿＿と消しゴム一＿＿＿＿＿＿＿下さい。
（け）

_____

_____

18. この教室の中に生徒が三十六＿＿＿＿＿＿＿います。先生は一＿＿＿＿＿＿＿です。
（きょうしつ）（せいと）

_____

_____

19. 今、雨が降っています。傘を二＿＿＿＿＿＿＿持って来て下さい。
（あめ）（ふ）（かさ）

_____

_____

20. 今、何時ですか。今、二＿＿＿＿＿＿＿四十九＿＿＿＿＿＿＿です。

_____

_____

21. 誕生日はいつですか。八＿＿＿＿＿＿＿十六＿＿＿＿＿＿＿です。
（たんじょうび）

_____

_____

四 Writing: Title your story "My Perfect Day"(私のパーフェクトな日). The particles you have learned so far are listed here. Write a paragraph (at least 6 sentences) about your ideal day, using each of the particles below at least once each. Number each particle as you use it the first time to make sure you include all 12 particles. Be creative, but don't be too crazy! Use as many 漢字 as possible. Include information about:

- the perfect weather （天気）
- the perfect amount of sleep （寝る事）
- the perfect meals （食べ物と飲み物）
- the perfect activities （趣味、する事）
- the perfect person to spend your ideal day with （一番いい友達といっしょに）

Particles: は、が、に、と、か、から (from)、でも、まで、を、も、の、で

_____

_____

_____

_____

_____

_____

_____

_____

_____

_____

_____

_____

_____

_____

名前：   日付：   月   日

― Translate the following sentences using *kanji* and *kana*.

1. My hobby is singing. (use 事) _____

2. I ate breakfast at 7:30. _____

3. I haven't yet eaten lunch. _____

4. Tomorrow it will probably rain. _____

＝ Translate each sentence into Japanese. Use the hints in parentheses in your answers. Pay special attention to the verb tense.

5. Yesterday my head hurt. (〜かった)

    _____

6. I love skiing, but I hate playing basketball. (する事)

    _____

7. Do you have a larger one? (もっと)

    _____

8. Next month it will probably be hot. (でしょう)

    _____

9. I am skilled at dancing. (得意)
           とく い

    _____

10. My little brother is not yet a middle school student. (まだ)

    _____

11. My mother has been living in London, but now she is in Tokyo. (〜が、)

    _____

12. My high school's baseball team is really strong this year. (強い)

    _____

三 Read Billy's self introduction and answer the questions below in English.

僕の　名前は　ビリーです。高校二年生で、十七歳です。スケボーを　する事が
大好きです。でも、まだ　上手ではありません。どこでも、いつでも、スケボー
が　したいです。でも、学校で　スケボーをしては　いけません。毎日、学校の
後、スケボーを　持って、公園まで行って、三人の　友達と　練習をします。公
園は　学校から　近いです。今は　スケボーは　まだ　ちょっと下手ですが、来
年は　スケボーの　国際大会へ　行ってみたいです。がんばります！

13. How old is Billy? What grade is he in? _____

14. What is his hobby? _____

15. Where does he practice his hobby? _____

16. How far is this practice site from his school? _____

17. Does he practice his hobby at school? _____

18. With whom does he practice his hobby? _____

四 Short writing: Respond to Jun's text message in Japanese. Use as many kanji as you can, and be sure to answer all his questions.

こんにちは。お元気ですか。僕は　毎日　いそがしいです。あなたも　いそが
しいですか。それとも、暇ですか。来週は　大事な　*入学試験が　あります。
今、一生懸命　勉強しています。来年は　大学に　行きたいです。あなたの
学校は　学期末*に　しけんが　ありますか。むずかしいですか。あなたは
来年、何をしたいですか。

じゃあね。
じゅん

* 入学試験 – entrance exam; 学期末 – end of the semester

_____

_____

_____

_____

名前：　　　　　　　　　　　　　　　　　日付：　　　月　　　日

➊ Translate the following sentences using *kanji* and *kana*.

1.   Please give me three sheets of paper.

   _____

2.   There are 2 people in the car.

   _____

3.   Open your textbook to page 173.

   _____

4.   Ben will be a 10th grader next year.

   _____

➋ Write the correct form of the adjective according to the English cue.

5.   あの_____本は　だれのですか。
   To whom does that blue book belong?

6.   先週の天気は　_____ですね。
   The weather last week was hot, wasn't it?

7.   私の家は　_____。
   My house is not quiet.

8.   明日は　_____。
   あした
   Tomorrow will probably be cool.

9.   前は、あの水泳のチームは_____が、今は_____。
   まえ　　　　　すいえい
   That swimming team was strong before, but now they aren't strong.

Use this list of adjectives to write sentences as directed below. Do not use any adjective more than once. Write the English translation under your Japanese sentence.

い adjectives		な adjectives	
忙しい （いそが）	遠い （とお）	きれい	静か （しず）
大きい	長い （なが）	有名 （ゆうめい）	元気 （げんき）
低い （ひく）	赤い （あか）	不思議 （ふしぎ）	じゃま
難しい （むずか）	弱い （よわ）		
高い （たか）	美味しい （おい）		

10. (non-past affirmative)
     い adjective sentence : _____

     English translation   : _____

     な adjective sentence : _____

     English translation   : _____

11. (past affirmative)
     い adjective sentence : _____

     English translation   : _____

     な adjective sentence : _____

     English translation   : _____

12. (non-past negative)
     い adjective sentence : _____

     English translation   : _____

     な adjective sentence : _____

     English translation   : _____

13. (past negative)
     い adjective sentence : _____

     English translation   : _____

     な adjective sentence : _____

     English translation   : _____

㊃ Write the *kanji* stroke order below with the first stroke in the first box, the first and second stroke in the second box, etc. Fill in any remaining boxes in that row with the same *kanji* and the blank rows at the bottom with other *kanji* you need to practice.

母
父
兄
弟
姉
妹
家
赤
青
黒
白
茶
色

五 Write the English translations in the crossword puzzle (you do not need to leave a space between words).

Across (横)
4. 小さかったです。
5. 長くなかったです。
8. 静かです。
9. 紫
11. 美しい

Down (縦)
1. きいろ
2. うれしくないです。
3. 青かったです。
6. きらい
7. きたない
10. つまらなくない

名前：   日付：   月   日

● Translate the following sentences using *kanji* and *kana*.

1. Please listen to this song. _____

2. May I go to my locker? _____

3. My younger sister is studying math. _____

4. The flowers are 2,500 yen. _____

● Fill in the correct verb tense according to the English translation. The dictionary form of the verb you need to conjugate is provided in the parentheses.

5. 私は、天ぷらと、巻き寿司に _____。（する）
   I'll have the tenpura and the makizushi.

6. 明日、五ドルを _____。（もって来る）
   Please bring $5 tomorrow.

7. 僕は　太郎君を家から学校に _____。（連れて行く）
   I will take Taro from my house to school.

8. 私は、校長先生に _____。（会う）
   I want to meet with the school principal.

9. でも、図書館には、_____。（行く）
   But, I don't want to go to the library.

10. 金曜日の午後四時にテニスを_____か。（する）
    Won't you play tennis with me on Friday at 4 p.m.?

11. 父は犬に水を _____。（やる）
    My father gave some water to the dog.

12. 私は、おばさんから大きいプレゼントを_____。（もらう）
    I received a large present from my aunt.

13. トム君は私の兄に風船と誕生日カードを_____。（くれる）
    Tom gave balloons and a birthday card to my older brother.

14. 私は、先生から美しい字の手紙を _____。（いただく）
    I received a beautifully written letter from my teacher.

Yooko invited Sam to a party at a restaurant last weekend. He was excited about attending, but he did not have as much fun as he anticipated. Here are several things Sam wrote in his journal before the party. Change the statements he wrote before the party into "after-the-party" (past negative tense) statements.

> **例** ようこさんのパーティーへ行きたいです。→
> <u>ようこさんのパーティーへ行きたくなかったです。</u>

15. レストランの食べ物は美味しいです。→

_____

16. ようこさんの友達と会います。→

_____

17. ゲームをします。→

_____

18. 風船と花火があります。→

_____

19. アイスクリームとケーキをいただきます。→

_____

20. レストランは近いです。→

_____

21. パーティーは楽しいです。→

_____

名前 :

日付 :　　　　月　　　日

➊ Translate the following sentences using *kanji* and *kana*.

1. The party was July 29, 2009.

   _____

2. My mother and my father are in Shikoku.

   _____

3. Last week I took my friend to Yokohama.

   _____

4. Mr. Yamamoto (teacher) took his class to Nagasaki.

   _____

➋ Write each sentence in Japanese. Use as many *kanji* as you can.

5. My father speaks Japanese and Chinese.

   _____

6. I was born in February 1986 in Tokyo.

   _____

7. Every day I wake up, eat, and go to school.

   _____

8. What is your favorite drink?

   _____

9. Please look with (by means of) your eyes and listen with (by means of) your ears.

   _____

10. How will the weather be tomorrow? It will probably rain.

   _____

11. I said, "What is your name?"

_____

12. In front of my house are a pond, white flowers, and 3 trees.

_____

≡ Your friend Rie sent you an e-mail invitation to a party. Unfortunately, she forgot to change the *hiragana* into *kanji*, and you are having a hard time understanding the invitation. Write the correct *kanji* just above the underlined *hiragana* below. Then refer to the invitation to answer the questions below in English.

招待状

たかだ　こうこう　にねんせいの　なつの　プール・パーティー

日付　　：にせんじゅうにねん　しちがつ　にじゅうごにち

じかん　：ごご　いちじはん　から　ごご　はちじ　まで

場所　　：たかだ　こうこうの　プール

もってくるもの：みずぎ (bathing suit)；タオル；すきな　のみもの；

　　　　　　　　プールの　ゲーム　ひとつ；がっこうの　せんせいた

　　　　　　　ちは　たべものを　もってきてくれます。BBQで

　　　　　　　す。はなびもします！

RSVP：やまもと　りえ

でんわ　：027-53-0111

13. What sort of party will this be?

_____

14. Who will be attending?

_____

15. What do you need to bring?

_____

16. Do you need to bring food?

_____

17. Why or why not?

_____

_____

_____

_____

18. Name two activities that will be going on at the party.

_____

19. Will you attend?

_____

20. Why or why not?

_____

_____

_____

_____

名前：　　　　　　　　　　　　　　　　　　　　　　日付：　　　月　　　日

🔊 Listen to the prompts and choose the best response for the following questions.

Two high school students, one from the U.S.A. and one from Great Britain, are just about to return to their countries after a year as exchange students in Japan. They are talking about all the various things they did while in Japan.

1. What sport did Paul mention seeing in Japan?
   a. soccer   b. sumo
   c. judo   d. baseball

2. What did Linda like best about Japan?
   a. the food   b. her school
   c. her home stay   d. the mountains

3. Does Linda want to return?
   a. yes, but not right away   b. yes
   c. no, she wants to go to China first   d. no

4. Linda wants to become a/an:
   a. Japanese teacher in Britain   b. English teacher in Britain
   c. Japanese teacher in Japan   d. English teacher in Japan

5. What does Paul think about Linda's idea?
   a. he says it sounds crazy   b. he says it sounds interesting
   c. he says it sounds difficult   d. he says it sounds great

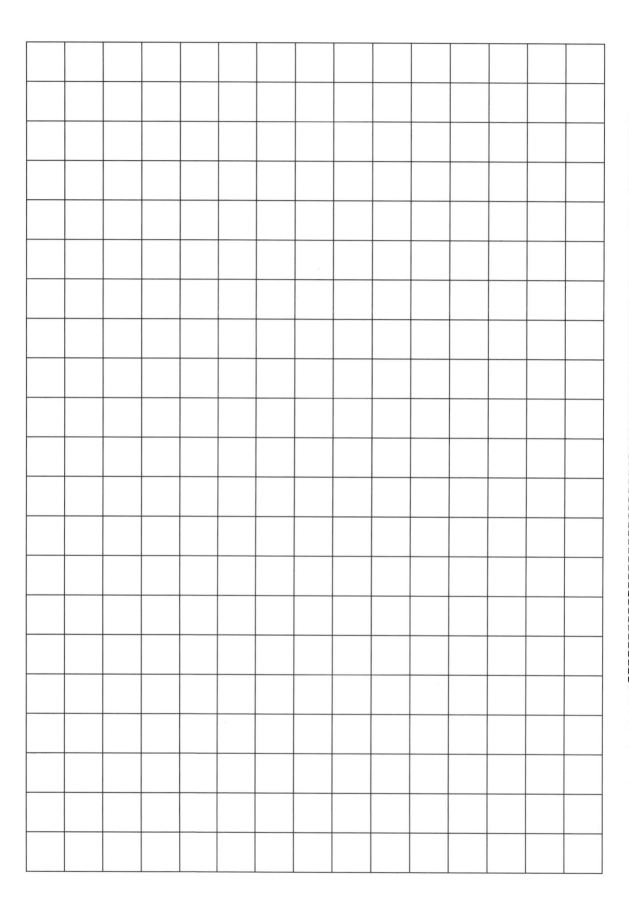

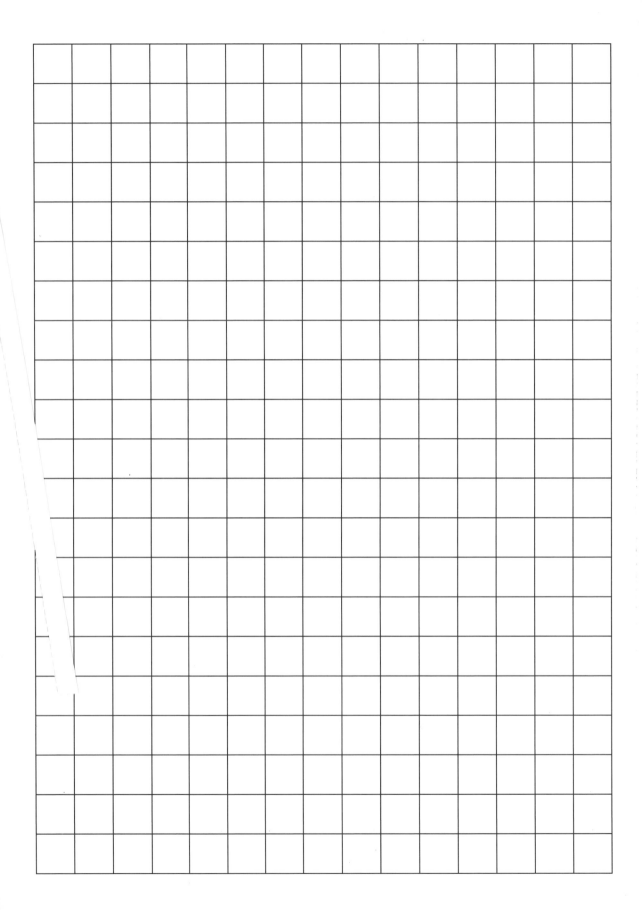

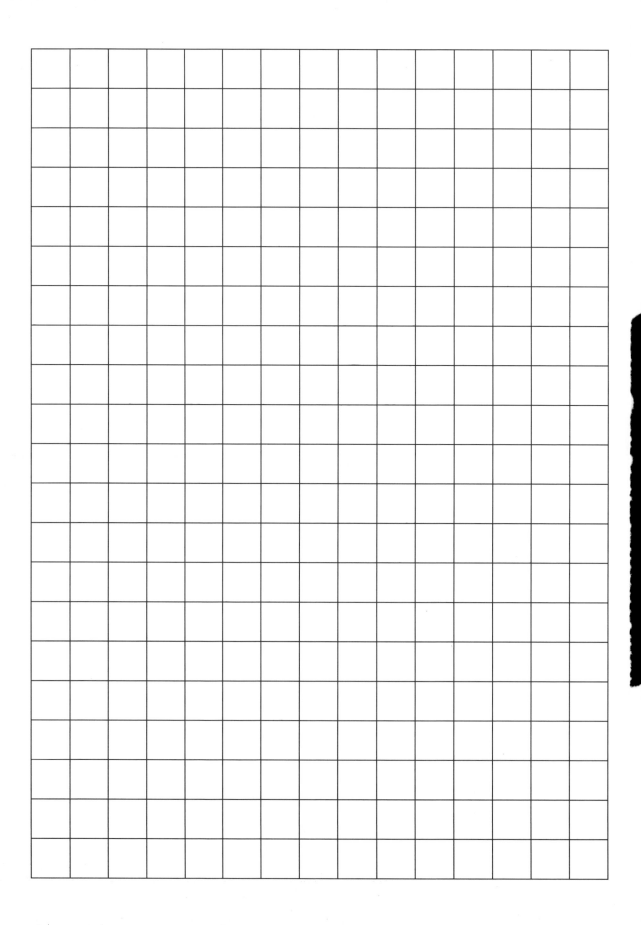